HALFCOURT®
BASKETBALL

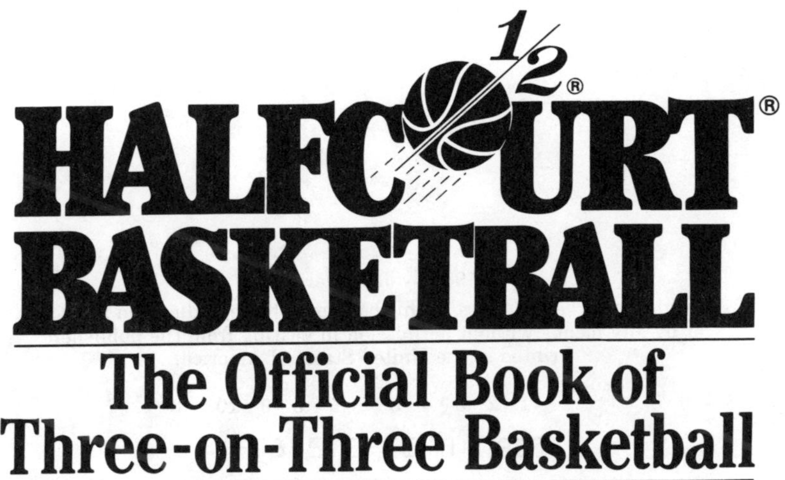

HALFCOURT BASKETBALL

The Official Book of Three-on-Three Basketball

Jack Herschlag

Prentice-Hall, Inc., Englewood Cliffs, New Jersey 07632

Library of Congress Cataloging in Publication Data

Herschlag, Jack.
Halfcourt basketball.

Includes index.
1. Halfcourt basketball. I. Title.
GV887.H48 1984 796.32′3′02022 83-27238
ISBN 0-13-372087-X
ISBN 0-13-372079-9 (A Reward book : pbk.)

1 2 3 4 5 6 7 8 9 10

ISBN 0-13-372087-X

ISBN 0-13-372079-9 {A REWARD BOOK : PBK.}

Editorial/production supervision:
Joe O'Donnell Jr. and Rita Young
Cover design: Hal Siegel
Cover illustration: Stephen Perry
Manufacturing buyer: Pat Mahoney

This book is available at a special discount when ordered in bulk quantities. Contact Prentice-Hall, Inc., General Publishing Division, Special Sales, Englewood Cliffs, N.J. 07632.

The photograph on page 62 is by Timothy Jones;
the photograph on page 78 is by Gerald Tietz;
and the photographs on pages 32, 56, and 72 are by Bert Rashby.

Prentice-Hall International, Inc., *London*
Prentice-Hall of Australia Pty. Limited, *Sydney*
Prentice-Hall Canada Inc., *Toronto*
Prentice-Hall of India Private Limited, *New Delhi*
Prentice-Hall of Japan, Inc., *Tokyo*
Prentice-Hall of Southeast Asia Pte. Ltd., *Singapore*
Whitehall Books Limited, *Wellington, New Zealand*
Editora Prentice-Hall do Brasil Ltda., *Rio de Janeiro*

Contents

Preface

This book is about Halfcourt® Basketball, the formalized version of three-on-three, one-basket basketball. Halfcourt® is played according to rules established by Halfcourt® Basketball Inc. (HBI), which was founded to serve as the headquarters, information center, and public voice of the sport.

HBI published its first rule book in 1977. Since then it has organized hundreds of programs throughout the United States in cooperation with municipalities, colleges, high schools, YMCA branches, summer camps, youth groups, fraternal organizations, and military bases. This experience is the reason for a number of rule changes that appear in this edition.

HBI's experience also has demonstrated the need for something more than a rule book, a book that would define Halfcourt® Basketball and the roles of all participants, including players, coaches, officials, and program directors, as well as the enormous career and recreation opportunities offered by this sport. This is the purpose of this book.

In these pages, the type of basketball played with one basket is referred to by the generic terms *one-basket basketball, one-hoop basketball, three-on-three basketball,* and the like. "Halfcourt" is used only in reference to the game played under the official rules of Halfcourt® Basketball Inc. "Halfcourt" is the registered trademark of Halfcourt® Basketball Inc.

Players, program directors, and other "role" types are sometimes referred to as "he" or "him." This style is used for brevity, and not for the purpose of diminishing the importance of females to Halfcourt® or Halfcourt® to females. The philosophy of

Halfcourt® basketball and the practices of Halfcourt® Basketball Inc. demonstrate that sexism is not one of the sins of this sport.

Acknowledgments

I wish to acknowledge the important contribution to Halfcourt® basketball made by Irving Gregory, a very special friend and colleague.

My special thanks to Rick Barry, who contributed portions of this book and who has given Halfcourt® basketball his continued help and encouragement over the years.

Many others have played key roles in the development of Halfcourt® basketball, including: Grady Armstrong, Salisbury State College, Salisbury, Maryland; Dr. Lloyd C. Arnold, National Council of the Young Men's Christian Associations of the United States; John Braune, Special Olympics, Inc.; Earl Davis of the International Association of Approved Basketball Officials, Anchorage, Alaska; Jim Haley, Vanguard High School, Ocala, Florida; Dell Husted, Athletic Director of the Mormon Church in the Anchorage, Alaska, area; James P. Miller, Daytona Beach Community College; Jim Purce, Washington, D.C., Department of Recreation; Bill Rawls, New York City Department of Parks and Recreation; Leonard Rosewarren, White Plains YMCA, White Plains, New York; and Joe Sacco, New York Military Academy, Cornwall-on-Hudson, New York.

Among the many outstanding sports and recreation administrators who have pioneered Halfcourt® basketball in their communities, the following have come to my attention: Jim Baurer, Murray State University, Murray, Kentucky; Dick de Bear, Over 40 Halfcourt® Basketball League, Plymouth, Michigan; Wes Evans, Canyonville Bible Academy, Canyonville, Oregon; Dave Fanucchi, Northwest Family YMCA, La Jolla, California; John Gedz, Oakbrook Terrace Community Park District, Villa Park, Illinois; Joe L. Jones, Cameron University, Lawton, Oklahoma; Phil Mandel, Independence Lodge No. 1776, B'nai B'rith, Greater Washington, D.C., Metropolitan Area; Dalton Overstreet, Eastern Arizona College, Thatcher, Arizona; Sue Perkins, Walla Walla College, College Place, Washington; Sam

Radel, Recreation Director, Woodville, Ohio; Richard Rozek, Burbank YMCA, Burbank, California; Robert Silverman, Camp Airy, Thurmont, Maryland; Craig Taylor, George Fox College, Newberg, Oregon; Natalie Tysz, Merrick Road Park Recreation Department, Merrick, New York; Johnny Walker Jr., Crenshaw Family YMCA, Los Angeles, California; Terry Warner, University of California, Santa Cruz, California; Reggie Williams, Felton Laboratory School, South Carolina State College, Orangeburg, South Carolina; and Robert Wilson III, Hampton Institute, Hampton, Virginia.

Two associates who have proven to be special friends of Halfcourt® basketball are Jim Ellison and John Laurence.

The affiliations listed above were in effect when the individuals named were most actively associated with Halfcourt® Basketball Inc. Titles have been omitted for the sake of brevity.

I offer my apologies to those who deserve to be acknowledged here but are not mentioned because of gaps in my records or recollection.

Introduction

To be a good full-court five-on-five player, you need to get your roots in three-on-three competition, because the game is basically situations involving three-on-three, two-on-two, and one-on-one.

I credit a great deal of my success in basketball to the schooling I received as a youngster from my dad. It was his procedure to involve us in three-on-three basketball. That was the way I learned the game.

For pure fun, excitement, and a good workout, you can't beat three-on-three basketball. For that reason, it's popular from the formative ages through middle age, and for some people, even beyond that. Through the formation of HBI, I feel we will provide an opportunity for the unsung heroes to get the recognition they truly deserve. After all, more people play one-basket basketball than full court.

Rick Barry
Commissioner, Halfcourt® Basketball

To the millions of anonymous players who created the game.

1

Halfcourt® from the Beginning

A basketball junkie will play the game wherever there is a ball and a hoop.

A ball and *a* hoop? One hoop?

That's right, just one. And here we have one of the great mix-ups in sports. The game James Naismith invented called for *two* baskets, one at each end of the court. The game invented by the players when Dr. Naismith wasn't around called for one basket, located anywhere at all. That's as much difference as there is between softball and baseball, or between one-wall and four-wall handball, yet both games are called basketball.

COMPARISONS BETWEEN FULL COURT BASKETBALL AND HALFCOURT® BASKETBALL

FULL COURT BASKETBALL

1. The court: Two facing baskets at opposite ends of a rectangular court measuring up to 50′ x 94′.

a. When the ball changes hands, there is an interval in the offensive action during which the team in possession brings the ball into its forecourt.
b. The fast break is a major offensive weapon. This consists basically of a footrace from one end of the court to the other.
c. Games can be played only where there are two facing baskets in place.

2. The team: Five players on the court

a. The five-man team dictates a great degree of specialization. Forwards and centers are required to be tall;

guards are required to be quick, good ball handlers, and good shooters. There are also offensive and defensive specialists. Generally, each player is assigned a floor area appropriate to his function.

b. The concentration of five defensive players within the field goal area makes a zone defense effective in full court basketball. However, the zone defense reduces action and interest so drastically that it has been outlawed in National Basketball Association competition.

c. Most offensive plays involve no more than three players. This means that 40 percent of the players on the court are out of the action at any given time.

3. Equipment and personnel: Clocks, referees, scorers, etc.

Full court basketball normally requires two on-court officials, a timekeeper, a scorekeeper, a special clock to time the quarters, a scoreboard, buzzers, and sometimes additional equipment if a 24-second or 30-second rule is in effect.

HALFCOURT® BASKETBALL

1. The court: One basket on a rectangular court half the size of a full court.

a. The ball is always within field goal range, which virtually eliminates the interval in offensive action when the ball changes hands.

b. The fast break is replaced by other strategies that depend more on ball handling than running speed or stamina. These strategies are unique to Halfcourt®.

c. Games can be played wherever there is a single basket. The practical implications of this difference between full court and Halfcourt® are enormous, in view of the millions of single-basket facilities that exist in playgrounds, backyards, etc.

2. The team: Three players on the court

a. All playing roles are interchangeable, which shifts the emphasis from specialization to versatility. Players operate on all parts of the court.

b. The distribution of three defensive players within the field goal area presents each player with so great a zone to defend that the zone defense is rendered impracticable. Halfcourt® is primarily a "man-to-man" game.

c. All players are directly involved in virtually all plays.

3. Equipment and personnel: One official, one clock

Halfcourt® basketball can be played with one Official and an ordinary clock.

Even today, as we approach the basketball centennial, the confusion in terminology persists—not only among journalists, administrators, and casual observers, but also among the players themselves, who respond to various surveys by listing themselves as "basketball" players, regardless of the kind of basketball they play.

From the beginning, basketball has been two games, the public full court game and the anonymous, grass-roots one-basket game. The former has been codified on a national and international basis by rules committees for each level of competition, from high school to Olympics to professional. The latter is the invention of the people who play it, redefined in every neighborhood where it is played.

Yet, for all its local flavor, one-basket basketball is remarkably consistent. Once you know whether you're playing Taking It Back or Straight Up, there's not much more you need to ask.

Under the Straight Up system, any player may attempt a field goal whenever and wherever he gets his hands on the ball, even when he's just grabbed a defensive rebound under the basket. It's a leaper's game, very big in the inner city.

Taking It Back means that a player capturing a defensive rebound has to pass or dribble the ball back behind a predetermined line (usually the foul line) before anyone on his team can shoot. Taking It Back is closer to full court basketball than Straight Up in that it involves more teamwork and set plays.

Some other rule variations are described in the following paragraphs.

Losers' Out versus Winners' Out

In Losers' Out, the team that's scored upon gets possession. In Winners' Out, the team that scores keeps the ball. That's the macho way; if you want the ball, you've got to get it.

Free Pass

The free-pass rule means that a throw-in may not be intercepted. This is the fastest and surest way to get the ball into play, and is especially popular among beginners. Usually, the free-pass system also includes a rule that forbids the receiver of the throw-in to shoot.

Double Pass

The double pass and "everyone touches" systems are designed to keep one player from hogging the ball. They also prevent a team from protecting a weak player. If butterfingers is forced to handle the ball, he'll either learn how to protect it or cost his team in turnovers.

As you wander from neighborhood to neighborhood looking for a game, you'll run into inconsistencies that are caused not by local customs but by local conditions. These come under the heading of ground rules. One-basket basketball has lots of these rules because it is played in the most makeshift facilities imaginable—backyards, driveways, parking lots, dead-end streets, and such, as well as conventional playgrounds, gyms, and schoolyards. Here are some of the ground rules you can expect to run into:

> "The fence is out."
> "The *second* yellow line is out."
> "If it hits the crack, we keep playing."
> "If it hits the curb, whoever touched the ball last takes it out."

Full court basketball is primarily an indoor game (*Webster's New Collegiate Dictionary defines* it as such), but one-hoop basketball is played everyplace, so the local legislators of its ground rules must take all environments into account:

> "Off the ceiling is out."
> "If it goes into the puddle, we choose."
> "If it hits the branch, we keep playing."

The most common outdoor ground rule concerns the upright pole that supports the basket. The universal rule is that if the ball hits the pole, it is out of bounds. There are subclauses to deal with players swinging on the pole, climbing it, pushing off against it, or using it for a "pick."

One ground rule has nothing to do with the court at all. Perhaps it shouldn't even be called a ground rule, but a fact of life. I'm referring to the number of players per team. Three players (three-on-three) is considered ideal because it allows for all the possibilities of basketball team play—screens, blocks, give-and-go, and so on—without crowding the court. Sometimes, when you have fewer than six players, you go with the bodies on hand. If there are too many players, the left-outs either wait to play the winners or look for another game.

Organizing a one-hoop game is an exercise in political science. Take a situation where there are seven players waiting for a three-on-three game. How do you eliminate the odd man? The democratic way is to shoot foul shots. The first three to make it comprise the first team. The second three make up the second team. The seventh man waits for winners.

While pure democracy guarantees impartiality, it does not guarantee even sides. Representative democracy does: The first two players to make free throws become, in effect, the team captains, and each selects his two teammates. First choice goes to the one who hit the first free throw. Then there's the tribal system, with each team showing up as a unit and always playing together, and the dictatorship, with the two toughest dudes on the court declaring themselves captain and choosing their teammates by conscription.

However, in most cases, you've got to make a free throw to play. That's heavy incentive. Imagine benching a full court player every time he misses a foul shot!

Winning offers the same incentive, not just for the individual but for the whole team. If you win, you get to play the next game. The proudest boast of any three-on-three star is, "I stayed on the court all day." What an incentive for team play! The hot dog who blows a game because of his one-man theatrics will hear it from his pals as they sit out the next game together. How long they sit is determined by how many other teams are waiting and how many baskets it takes to win, because three-on-three is always played against a point total. Depending on local custom, it could be eleven points, fifteen, twenty-one, or any number, usually with the provision that you have to win by two. If several teams are waiting, the point total will be set low to give everyone a chance to play. Moreover, there is often a "shut-out" provision, meaning that a seven-to-nothing score ends the game right there.

One of the arts of playground ball is learning the turf. A smart three-on-three player will locate the dead spots on the backboard. He'll know which rims are "tight" and which are either too low or too high. He'll know where the sun is and force his opponent to shoot into it. He'll give his man the outside shot in a high wind. He'll try to pick the game ball that suits him best—light or heavy, dead or lively, new or bald.

The real personality of one-basket basketball comes through in the way fouls and violations are called. The standard procedure is for each player to make his own calls. If the ball touches the line or the pole, anyone on the opposing team calls it. If someone is fouled, *he* makes the call. If someone is fouled and his teammate makes the call, protocol requires the other team to tell him, "Mind your own business."

Inevitably there are disagreements. Sometimes one opinion prevails. More often there is a stand-off, in which case the universal arbiter is called in—the choose.

The choose takes the place of officials, jump balls, and fisticuffs. One player calls "odds," the other calls "evens," and at a given signal they each flick out either one finger or two. The sum of the fingers determines who is right. Many citizens of the blacktop believe that winning a choose means they really *are* right. Others learn to take justice into their own hands, literally, and they become quite skillful at choosing.

On rare occasions, a player involved in a dispute will appeal to higher authority, someone waiting for winners. His answer from the figure leaning against the fence will always be the same: "I wasn't watching."

The sum of all these subtleties is that, one way or another, the game goes on. I have watched and participated in thousands upon thousands of one-hoop games and can't recall a half dozen times when an argument broke up a game, but I can remember sneaking into closed gyms, climbing storm fences, shoveling away snow, braving the attacks of security guards, and enduring "skins and shirts" in frigid weather just to play some three-on-three.

My contention is that virtually 100 percent of all basketball players play the one-basket game, while a much smaller percentage play full court. Many surveys on basketball inquire *only* into organized full court basketball. This leaves us with the anomaly that, statistically, the number of people playing *one-hoop* basketball is greater than the number playing *all* of basketball.

Halfcourt® Basketball Inc. has gathered together the results of several surveys designed to determine the popularity of various sports and the number of people participating in each. Generally, they rank "basketball" as number one among team sports, ahead of baseball, football, softball, and soccer, but behind certain individual activities, like swimming. Jogging, another individual sport, is ahead of basketball in some surveys and behind in others. One survey of "fitness activities" includes such solo pastimes as walking and calisthenics, and both are rated more popular than basketball. Tennis and bowling, which are primarily individual sports, usually rank somewhere close to basketball. In sum, basketball is America's leader among team sports.

Upwards of 20 million people play the game. By including all the uncountables—the preteens, the unaffiliated, the backyard aficionados, and the misclassified—the figure comes closer to 30 million. At least, this is what HBI believes.

The point of this exercise in numbers is not to demonstrate that "we're number one" but to point out that a very large sports-hungry segment of the population is being ignored. Recreation administrators use a better word—"underserved," which says it all. Facilities, equipment, personnel, time, and money are allocated to serve dozens of other sports, while three-on-three players go . . . underserved. The purpose of HBI is to turn this around, to give three-on-three recognition and organization, under the name of Halfcourt®, so that 30 million participants can find a home.

The history of one-hoop isn't entirely bleak. In the course of our research we found that here and there the playground tradition did come in out of the cold. Some YMCA branches started three-on-three programs for players who were cut from their regular basketball teams. Certain intramural directors recognized the need for a low-key alternate to full court basketball. Municipal recreation departments set up programs so youngsters could have scheduled playing time. And the "continuation" value of three-on-three for players beyond their mid-twenties led to programs for employees, military personnel, and over-forty diehards.

The people who pioneered these programs had to make up their own rules, for there was no central organizing body. Their efforts were rich in ingenuity. Here are some examples: What do you do when there aren't enough basketballs to go around? Here's one solution, in Rule 15 of the Merrick Road Park Recreation Department, Merrick, New York: "Basketballs will be provided by the individual teams."

How do you stop a team from delaying the game? This is how they do it in intramural competition at Brooklyn College: "After a warning by the Official to 'Play Ball,' the offensive team must make an attempt at the basket within 10 seconds."

Stetson University, in DeLand, Florida, dealt with delay of game a little differently: "Teams must play active offense and defense. Teams shall attempt to score. There will be no time limit but 24–30-second rule serves as the guideline. If there is a delay of game violation, a jump ball will take place."

Stetson also took a stand against the kind of lineup juggling that goes on in some sports when it ruled, "Substitutions may be made prior to a throw-in. However, no player may be removed for a substitute who has not participated in active play."

Organizers of three-on-three programs learned to get the game played despite all kinds of adverse situations. This is the way the Northwest Family YMCA of La Jolla, California, handled the problem of no-shows: "A team without three players may use someone else only with the consent of the opposing team, who shall select make-up players of their choice."

And the New York City Department of Recreation solved the problem of missing court markings as follows: "The throw-in spot will be behind what ordinarily would be the center court line. A chalk line is suggested where no center line exists."

The University of California at Santa Cruz brought this

playground practice into its intramurals: "Choice of 1st outs determined by do or die from top of key." To make things even, the same set of rules stated, "Team losing 1st outs has choice of skins or shirts."

Three-on-three Officials have always been in short supply. In some programs, like intramural three-man basketball at New Mexico State University, they were available only for the playoffs. During the regular schedule the rule was that "teams must honor each others' foul calls and every effort should be made to play the game fairly and avoid unnecessary fouls and roughness. Official supervisors will be on hand to resolve any disputes, if asked."

The Northwest Family Y, however, was not arbitration-minded. Its rule on foul calls was, "Fouls will be called by players. One call and it stands—no discussions." The same Y branch legislated held-ball debates out of existence like this: "Player first calling 'First Out' will receive the ball out of bounds. At the time of the next held ball, the other team will receive the ball out of bounds."

Program directors have had to decide between taking the ball back or playing "straight up." Most have favored taking it back—but back to where? The free throw line? The free throw line extended? The back of the key? What's the penalty for *not* taking it back? For its over-thirty league, the Southern Hills Y of Brecksville, Ohio, laid down a very firm rule and a severe penalty: "When the ball changes possession from one team to another, the team with the ball must take the ball through the center circle before they can shoot. If they do not, and a shot is taken and made, the defensive team is awarded the basket, and the ball." Another key decision is whether to play Losers' Out or Winners' Out. B'nai B'rith Independence Lodge No. 1776, Washington D.C., opted for the latter, in these words: "Offense keeps possession as long as it scores (make it, take it)."

HBI drew upon the experience of recreation leaders and the grass-roots wisdom of the playground in formulating its own rules. The most important contribution of HBI was the introduction of the Official—the man with the whistle—into three-on-three basketball.

In February 1977, Halfcourt® Basketball Inc., was incorporated and the first rule book was published. During the following years, thousands of individuals entered the Halfcourt® network, delighted to find that their local pastime was emerging as an immensely popular national sport. HBI, the source of Halfcourt® material and information, provided a connection with other players and administrators who shared their interest in the sport. Following the introduction of the HBI rule book, which was distributed free of charge, some 200 programs were run using Halfcourt® rules and materials. Many were modified to accommodate local problems, while others were full-fledged Halfcourt® tournaments, Officials and all.

It was during this developmental period, in early 1979, that Rick Barry became commissioner of Halfcourt® Basketball. Rick was then a year away from retirement as one of the greatest basketball players of all time and was making plans for his post-playing career. One day in New York, before a game between the Houston Rockets and the New York Knicks, Rick was introduced to the Halfcourt® basketball idea. He was invited to become Halfcourt® commissioner, and he accepted.

While Halfcourt® was growing, HBI was learning. Feedback from the field led to innovations and refinements. The original elaborate Halfcourt® scorecard gave way to the concise official scorecard now in use, and the two-shirt uniform system was developed. In that system, an entire program is outfitted by giving each player two shirts, one in a "home" color and one in an "away" color, say red and gold. This enables any two teams to suit up for a game in contrasting uniforms, and the league doesn't have to go through the hassle and expense of finding twenty colors for twenty teams.

Halfcourt® also gained recognition in the educational and officiating communities. The HBI concept became part of the curriculum for physical education and recreation majors at several colleges, and officials welcomed Halfcourt® basketball as an easy sport to work and productive of career opportunities.

By far the most important lessons learned by HBI concerned the Halfcourt® rules. In an attempt to straddle the line between uniformity and flexibility, the original rule book offered some alternate rules, with this explanation:

> The first consideration of HBI is to get the game played. No rule or guideline in this book should be thought of as an obstacle. In this spirit, there are many alternate rules suggested to enable the game to go on under irregular conditions. These or any other alternate rules are official if both teams agree to them.

Although the motivation may have been laudable, the idea of alternate rules raised some valid objections. Rick Barry, for one, who is well known for having strong opinions about officiating, felt that alternate rules tended to generate controversy. The case against alternatives was summed up persuasively by James P. Miller, program manager of Parks, Recreation & Leisure Services at Daytona Beach Community College and past president of the Central Florida Officials Association. He felt that too many alternatives provided room for confusion and that the alternatives could lead to misunderstandings when interleague play is expected. Also, alternatives create confusion for Officials, who have to make split-second decisions yet may have to figure out which league supports which alternative before deciding.

Miller went on to explain, "A major problem in this community is acquiring competent flag football officials. The regular officials are refusing to work recreation league games due to the fact that of the five city departments in this coastal area there are five different variations in rules."

The advice of Rick Barry, James P. Miller, Earl Davis of Anchorage, Alaska, and others contributed much of the thinking that went into the revised rules. They deserve the gratitude of all who will benefit by participating in a greatly improved game. For the record, it should be said that in developing Halfcourt®, HBI has changed only what needed to be changed and preserved all that was effective and exciting in three-on-three. Anyone familiar with the schoolyard game will recognize in Halfcourt® the same stylized moves, the same intricate teamwork, the same gang-up under the board for every rebound, the same shooting virtuosity, and the same balance of intensity and goodwill.

Everything is in place to allow for the growth of Halfcourt® basketball into a major sport, serving players of every level of competence throughout their active careers, from preteen through middle age. Halfcourt® will grow as an intramural, extramural, and interscholastic sport. It will find its place in community, industrial, military, scouting, and fraternal programs. It will enjoy training, coaching, scholarships, and media attention. And Halfcourt® will play an important role in providing equal sports opportunities for women.

There is every reason to hope for annual Halfcourt® championship tournaments and professional teams, and even the possibility that Halfcourt® will gain the same Olympic recognition that has been granted to many less popular sports. Meanwhile, Halfcourt® is certain to continue as a breeding ground for full court players and as the game millions choose to play wherever there is a ball and a hoop.

2

The Player's Guide to Halfcourt® Basketball

You've been playing three-on-three basketball ever since you could bounce a ball, and you've always considered it your game. Well, it *is* your game. You've helped build it, along with millions of other players, into the most popular team sport in America.

Now it's your turn. Out of three-on-three has come Halfcourt® basketball, the organized version of one-basket basketball, with its own worldwide headquarters, Halfcourt® Basketball Inc. The purpose of HBI is not to take away from informal three-on-three but to add something to it. The playground game will surely go on, with the new role of preparing players for organized Halfcourt®. Here are some things you can do to become a good Halfcourt® player.

PLAYING TIPS

Free Throws

You never shot free throws before in a three-on-three game, but in Halfcourt® the free throw is an important weapon. So get to be an expert from the line, using these tips from Rick Barry, commissioner of Halfcourt® Basketball, who is the all-time free throw champion of the National Basketball Association.

> Practice as long and as often as you can. The more practice you have behind you the more automatic your shot becomes. To be successful in anything you must have confidence in your abilities and there's no better way to achieve that than to practice.

Remember to bend your knees. It is difficult to control the ball when you're shooting stiff-legged.

Learn to give your shot some height, or soft arc. This gives the ball a better downward angle and a better chance of dropping in if it catches the rim. A line drive shot that hits the rim tends to bounce away or spin in and out.

When taking aim, focus your eyes on the exact center of the front rim, and picture the ball dropping just over that part of the rim.

A little backspin on the ball will keep your shot on course and also help it drop in if it touches iron. However, don't exaggerate your shot to get the backspin.

Learn to take your time and relax. Bounce the ball a few times before you shoot if that seems to help, and take a deep breath to remove tension. Try to prepare yourself for each shot the same way each time.

If possible get in a few practice shots before each game with the ball that will be used in the game. There are often slight variations in the height of the basket, the feel of the ball, etc., and getting accustomed to them will help your accuracy.

Many people have asked me about my underhand free throw method. My answer to them and you is to shoot the shot you have the most confidence in, and remember that unless you can make 80 percent of your free throws, you are not a good free throw shooter. So practice, practice, practice. You can do it if you want to.

The Halfcourt® Fast Break

Under HBI rules, when you capture a rebound off the other team's shot, you must take the ball back behind the free throw line before your team can shoot. Getting this done quickly, before the opposing team sets up its defense, is a Halfcourt® fast break. This maneuver can create opportunities for easy baskets, just as the full court fast break does, but it depends more on passing and alertness than on running speed. For that reason you can keep on improving and refining your fast break skills, no matter how young or old you are.

In a Halfcourt® basketball program, you will be playing continuously with the same players, and that will give you an opportunity to practice your fast break as a team, to set up plays that can get the ball behind the foul line and back under the basket in two quick passes. You'll have to learn to vary your fast break, too, or an alert opponent will anticipate your pass and intercept it.

Following Your Shot

With only six players on the court, the player taking a shot has an excellent chance to retrieve his own rebound without getting boxed out. If you develop quickness at following your own shot, you can often create a three-on-two advantage for your team. And you can go right up with the ball, whereas the defensive team can't.

One way to improve your follow-up is to develop a standing jump shot. Most players will fake a defender into the air, then go up for a jumper while he's on his way down. You can vary this tactic by shooting from a standing position, *without* jumping, while the defender is on his way down. That way, as soon as the ball leaves your hands, you can take off for the follow-up.

The effectiveness of the standing jump shot is surprising to some players, because they assume they have to jump to clear the outstretched hands of the defender. However, unless he is considerably taller than you are, this is not necessarily true, because the element of surprise is in your favor.

There are other advantages to the standing jumper:

1. While the defender is in the air, you have the option to pass off and cut to the basket for a return pass (give and go).
2. You have better control of your shot.
3. You keep the option of faking a second time and taking a true jump shot.

Versatility

Halfcourt® requires every player to develop every skill, because each team has only three players on the court at any given time and the game is in constant flow. One moment you're on offense, the next you're on defense. One moment you're trying to get open for a pass, the next you're fighting for rebounding position. You can expect to be called upon to perform any role at any time. Therefore, to be a good Halfcourt® player, you have to be a *complete* player. During a lifetime of competition, you will certainly develop your own strengths, but you should never have any weaknesses. I'll give you some tips about developing a well-rounded game.

On offense, learn to move in any direction, with or without the ball, and learn to shoot from any spot. This does not mean that you won't have favorite moves or favorite spots, but it does mean that your defender will always have to take you seriously. He won't be able to drop off when you're out of your field goal range, and he won't be able to ignore your left hand and cheat to your right. By being "believable" with every move you make, you accomplish two things:

1. You make your strong points more effective, because the defender can't concentrate on them.
2. You take the pressure off your teammates, because your defender can't leave you to double up on someone else.

Passing

In all the basketball practice sessions you've ever seen, you may never have seen one devoted specifically to passing, yet for Halfcourt® this kind of training is highly recommended. The pass is your best weapon for pressuring the defense, creating openings, and taking advantage of scoring opportunities. It brings every player on your team into the offensive pattern.

Here are some passing tactics you can practice.

1. *Passing off the dribble.* Learn to take advantage of passing opportunities while you're dribbling. If a player on your team gets open for a shot while you are dribbling, you can't take time to stop and set yourself. The pass must come right off the dribbling motion. This is important not only for getting the ball to the open player quickly but also for minimizing the chances of your own defender's spotting the pass and blocking it.

There are ways to create scoring opportunities by passing off the dribble. For example, attract the attention of a teammate's defender by dribbling toward him. When he makes a move for the ball, your teammate cuts for the basket, and you scoop the ball to him.

To make use of this maneuver, and to be a good Halfcourt® player in general, you must learn to keep the whole court in view while you're dribbling. If you dribble with your head down, you've turned Halfcourt® into a one-player game. You won't spot the open player, and after a while your teammates will stop working for openings. Once they stop moving, they are giving the defense a chance to rest and allowing them to drop back for rebounds. Finally, there is nothing so boring as a game in which one player controls the ball while everyone else stands around.

2. *Passing while you're in the air.* When you go up for a jump shot and find that a defender is in your way, learn to pass off instead of shooting into a sure block. You should also learn to pass in midair off a rebound or interception, or when saving a ball that's going out of bounds. Work with your teammates on passing in any direction with either hand or both hands while your feet are off the floor.

3. *Blind passing.* Be deceptive with your eyes. Look one way and pass another so that the defensive team can never anticipate your pass. However, when you look away from the direction of your pass, you may be missing some movement by a teammate or defender. So don't pass to an area that has been out of your view for more than a split second. And work on your peripheral vision. Peripheral vision is the ability to see things off to the side when you're looking straight ahead. The farther to the side you can see, the wider your range of peripheral vision. Great basketball players are usually blessed with extraordinary peripheral vision, but most people have a greater range of side vision than they make use of. The keys to maximizing peripheral vision are discipline and self-confidence. Both can be developed by practice. When you spot something out of the corner of your eye, don't turn your head, but act on the information your eye gives you. Is it a teammate or an opponent, and which way is he moving? You don't need a full view to check this out, because peripheral vision is highly accurate on both movement and color.

4. *Passing behind the back.* Here's a typical game situation: You're controlling the ball with your right hand on the right side of the court while being closely guarded. One of your teammates gets free and heads down the free throw lane toward the basket. Your most protected way to get the ball to him is a behind-the-back pass, as it keeps your body between the ball and the player guarding you. Some players use this pass to show off, but that doesn't mean it doesn't have a legitimate role in Halfcourt®. So learn it, and use it at the proper time.

5. *The bounce pass.* There are at least two situations in which a bounce pass is preferable to an air pass: When you want the player receiving the pass to catch it rising as he goes up for a shot, and to minimize the possibility of interception when a defensive player is stationed along the passing lane.

In the second situation, aim your pass so that the ball touches the ground when it is nearest to the defensive player. This will force him to dive for it if he attempts an interception and thereby cut down his chances of reaching it. To make the interception still more difficult, you can aim the ball to touch the ground off to one side, away from the defender, and give it opposite spin to make it "come back" to the player receiving the pass.

6. *The lob pass.* This is your most dangerous pass, as it remains in the air for a long time. However, it does have a place in Halfcourt®, specifically in situations where you are leading a player who has a clear path to the basket and there is a defender blocking the passing lane. As a general rule, when throwing a lob pass, the closer the receiver is to the basket, the higher he should receive the ball.

Back Door Play

The back door play requires perfect teamwork, but when it works it is one of the most effective and beautiful plays in Halfcourt®. It depends on an offensive player without the ball getting inside position (between his defender and the basket) and causing the defender to turn his head away from the ball. At that moment the teammate with the ball throws him a lead pass, which is usually a lob or bounce pass. The role of the third offensive player is either to set up a block to help the shooter get free or to clear out to keep his defender out of the play. For the back door play to be successful, each player must know what his teammate is doing without voice or hand signals, so give it lots of practice.

Rebounding

Statistics show that most rebounds are taken below the level of the rim. This means that position is more important than jumping ability, and that's fortunate for the dedicated player, because your ability to gain position can be improved with practice. Here are some tips.

1. If you're a defender, you'll usually have the inside position (nearer the basket) on your opponent when the shot is taken. Learn to stay between him and the basket until you know which way the rebounding is going. At that point, start moving for the ball, but don't move directly under it before you jump. Keep back a bit to make your opponent "climb over" you, so that he will have less chance of grabbing the rebound and more chance of committing a foul.

2. Learn to tap rebounds. Tapping will "keep the ball alive" when you are unable to gain full control of it and enable you to keep the ball in the air and out of your opponent's hands while you set yourself for a second jump. You also can tap the ball to your teammate, in which case tapping takes the place of both rebounding and passing.

3. Develop an instinct for where the ball is going. If you're not fortunate enough to be born with that instinct, concentrate on certain clues that might tell you where the ball is going. For example, a low line-drive shot has a tendency to bounce hard off the rim. Soft, high shots often fall short.

4. Get used to the physical aspects of competing for position. In top-level full court basketball, the area around the basket is known as "no-man's-land," meaning that the referee will tolerate a lot of contact. Halfcourt® is stricter about contact, but there is still a gray area concerning who has the right to a particular spot on the court. The trick is to plant both feet on the ground for

maximum traction and to crouch a little to give yourself a low center of gravity. Then, when bodies collide, you'll have more pounds going for you than your actual weight.

Often you can use an opponent's own body against himself. If he has inside position, just brace yourself as he leans back against you, then step aside. As he struggles to regain his balance, you can move past him and take over the inside.

Defense

Halfcourt® defense is basically man-to-man. There's too much court for three players to cover to allow for an effective zone defense. However, some aspects of zone strategy can be useful:

1. When one defensive player "commits" himself on an attempted steal, he risks the possibility of missing the ball and leaving his opponent open. In anticipation of this, the defensive player farthest from the ball should move into the area between the ball and the basket, where he has the best chance of breaking up a scoring attempt.
2. There are times when the defense will "double-team" (use two defenders on) an offensive player. For example, when the offensive player with the ball is trapped in a corner, double-teaming him is a good way to force a wild pass. In such a situation, the third defensive player either gambles and heads into the most likely passing lane for a steal or drops back into a one-player zone.

In most situations, however, your primary defensive assignment will be to keep one player from scoring. Here are some tips on that.

1. When the man you're guarding has the ball, keep your hands extended, either up or out to the sides. This is your basic position of readiness. It provides balance and gives you a split-second edge on blocking shots and passes, and it interferes with your opponent's line of vision.
2. Concentrate on *not* going for the fake. Your opponent may

have a big arsenal of moves designed to make you commit yourself. Study them carefully. Try to sort out the real from the deceptive.

In general, focus your eyes on the middle of your opponent's stomach. If that spot moves, he has shifted his weight and you can shift with him. Even if the move is a fake, he's committed himself and has to recover to change his direction, just as you do.

3. If your opponent favors one hand when he dribbles, you can "cheat" to that side when he has the ball.

4. If your opponent has no outside shot, you can drop off him when he is beyond his range to handle some other defensive chore.

5. If your opponent favors one spot for shooting, force him out of that area. Head him off when he is moving in that direction. Make him take the bad percentage shot, or none at all.

6. Be aggressive. Don't allow the offensive player always to make the first move. Use fake attempts at stealing and other surprise moves to get *him* to think about *you*. That will distract him from his offensive game. He may also develop a pattern of reacting that can help you. For example, if he always reacts to your fake steal by switching the ball to his other hand, you can set him up for a steal by faking toward one side and moving toward the other.

7. Use teamwork on stealing. A typical two-player steal works like this: One defensive player makes a move at the ball while it is being dribbled. The dribbler spins away, not realizing that another defender has stepped in behind him and is waiting for the ball. In two-player steals, all you have to do is get one hand on the ball. You know where your teammate is and you just have to tap the ball to him.

Practice offensive plays off the steal. For example, if you've tapped the ball to your teammate, break immediately for the basket. The return pass will usually find you open for an easy shot.

8. Because in Halfcourt® the basket is always within shooting range, learn to make the transition from offense to defense instantaneously. Even when a ball is loose and possession is in

doubt, if you are away from the play your best bet is to move immediately for inside position. If your opponents get the ball, you're ready to defend. If your team gets it, you have the inside spot for a shot or rebound.

Blocks and Screens

A block is a maneuver performed by two offensive players. One player stands still while the other runs past him (with or without the ball) in such a way as to force his defender to stop, bump into, or move around the stationary player. There are many ways to use the block. When the moving player remains behind the stationary player to take a protected shot, the block is called a screen. Here are some other variations:

1. The player in movement draws both defenders to himself, and he passes back to the player setting the block.
2. The moving player passes the block, then stops and sets up a block for the first player to use.
3. Two players set up blocks for the third. This variation and variation 2 are designed to create confusion in the defense that will leave one offensive player uncovered.

Schoolyard players who are geared to one-on-one don't appreciate the value of blocks and screens, especially if they're the ones who have to set them up for others. But Halfcourt® is a team game, and blocks are an absolute necessity. So practice setting blocks and *thinking* blocks.

Dribbling

You'll do more passing than dribbling in Halfcourt®, but dribbling is still your most fundamental skill. Here is a list of goals to set for yourself in practicing the dribble.

1. Always protect the ball. Keep your body between the ball and your opponent as much as possible. This means dribbling

close to your body and learning to spin away from your defender and dribble behind your back.

2. Keep the ball low. A high bouncing dribble exposes the ball for a possible steal.

3. Learn to dribble with either hand. This gives you complete freedom to move in any direction, keeps your opponent guessing, and enables you to shield the ball with your body no matter which side of the court you are on.

4. Work on being as fast when you're moving with the ball as when you're without it.

5. When a ball is bouncing loose, learn to take possession with a dribbling motion. It's a good way to take advantage of an open lane to the basket. If you have to stop to grab the ball and then start again, the opportunity will be lost.

Moving without the Ball

Halfcourt® is a game of constant motion. When you're on offense, moving without the ball should become second nature. It will be instrumental in the following situations:

1. Setting up plays, like the back door play previously described. Or, a simple, sudden change of direction can get you open for a shot. Movement creates opportunities.

2. Wearing down your opponent. If you let him rest on defense, *he'll* wear *you* down on offense.

3. Keeping your defender's attention on you, so that he doesn't interfere with a play involving your two teammates and is less prepared to rebound.

Important: It's part of the rules of Halfcourt® that you must maintain offensive pressure. Since there's no twenty-four-second or thirty-second clock, the only way the Official can judge delay of game is if you're standing around, not working for scoring opportunities, or not taking advantage of scoring opportunities when you get them. So keep moving, and keep pressing to score.

Shooting

Attempting a field goal is nearly everyone's big moment in Halfcourt®, and the culmination of every offensive play. Practice your shooting every chance you get. Learn to shoot from the outside and from underneath. Learn to take lay-ups with either hand. Learn to shoot while jumping, running, and standing still. Learn to shoot when you're guarded, open, or behind a screen. Each kind of shot has its time and place, and when the opportunity arises, you should be ready for it.

However, none of the foregoing is intended to suggest that you shoot whenever you get your hands on the ball. After practicing *all* the shots, you'll be able to select which ones are your best, which are the ones that produce the highest percentage of field goals. During the game, those are the shots you should work for. This is what coaches mean when they talk about shot selection. They are talking about a player's self-discipline, his ability to forego a shot that he's not good at and stick to ones he has perfected.

Substitutions

Most players who have grown up with informal three-on-three are accustomed to playing an entire game without substitutions. Halfcourt® is different. There are two players ready to come in at any time. Often a substitution is made for strategic purposes, perhaps to improve the match-up against a particular opposing player. At other times substitutions can be made to give someone a rest. So get used to the idea that you don't have to "save yourself." You can go all out while you're in the game, then take a bench rest and come back in. If you're playing tired and your opponent is beating you on stamina, signal your coach to send in a replacement. This is one aspect of unselfish team play that wins games.

When you are on the bench, rest your body but not your mind. Keep your eyes on the game. Look for weaknesses in the other team that can be exploited. Look for weaknesses in your own team that have to be changed. And pay special attention to the player you will be covering on defense when you return to the court.

Dealing with Officials

Officiating is another aspect of Halfcourt® that playground ball doesn't prepare for you. In Halfcourt® you don't call your own fouls and violations. They're called by someone with a whistle, just as in full court basketball. Learn to accept his ruling as final; no arguing or "choosing." If you do argue, the Official has the option of calling a technical foul for delay of game. And he will be prone to do so, because Halfcourt® is played with running time, and every second counts. Also keep in mind that prolonged delay, or any other kind of unsportsmanlike conduct, can result in your disqualification. The Official has that option, too.

In full court basketball, players often debate a foul call because they are in danger of fouling out. It may be helpful to remember that there is no individual foul limit, and therefore no fouling out, in Halfcourt®. The reason is that by committing a foul in Halfcourt®, you *always* hurt your own team; you *never* gain an advantage. That's the way the rules are set up. So learn not to argue, and not to foul.

3

The Coach's Guide to Halfcourt® Basketball

Coaching Halfcourt® basketball offers some unusual challenges and rewards, particularly while the role of the coach is still being defined. Now and for years to come, each coach will be able to shape his own Halfcourt® style and create a tremendous difference in the performance of his team just by working on the fundamentals that three-on-three players often neglect.

Full court experience is a definite advantage to the Halfcourt® coach, but he can't be fully effective unless he recognizes two important practical distinctions between full court and Halfcourt®:

1. *A greater need for versatility.* In full court, a team can afford to carry a few specialists who concentrate on defense, rebounding, shooting, or some other narrow aspect of the game. In Halfcourt®, there are only three players on the court, and any one of them may be called upon to do any job at any time. There's no way to hide a weakness in Halfcourt®.

2. *The greater importance of the transitional game.* In full court, the need to move the ball from one end of the court to the other allows time for the offensive team to regroup into its defensive assignments. The only exception is the fast break. In Halfcourt®, the transition from offense to defense is almost instantaneous, as if every change of possession were a fast break, and players must be trained to react accordingly.

Obviously, developing versatility and teaching the transitional game have a lot to do with each other. For example, in switching from offense to defense, a player doesn't always have time to look for the opponent who is assigned to him. Often he will have to cover whomever is near. That requires a complete defensive arsenal. It means knowing how to cover both taller and shorter players, reacting correctly to all styles of faking, shooting, jumping, dribbling, and passing, and learning how to fight for position against players who use their bodies in many different ways.

This is more than a matter of preseason and pregame training. It is part of each game, and it requires each player to become familiar with every opponent on the court, not just "his man." One of the jobs of the coach is to build versatility into each player in a general way and to teach him to pay attention to the whole court during every game—when he is sitting on the bench as well as when he is playing.

CONDITIONING

In trying to match your team's strength against another's weakness, a very important consideration is conditioning. Each player on your five-man roster should be in top condition, and while on the court he should be able to apply continuous pressure, both on offense and defense. If he tires, he should be taught to signal to the bench for a substitute and not try to coast on the court. Constant movement will often reveal a weak spot in the opposition, a player who can't keep up with the action. When that happens, the strategy is to work every play in that player's direction, to gain field goal opportunities, draw fouls, and perhaps force an advantageous substitution.

In applying offensive pressure, the pass is a superior weapon to the dribble, because you don't have to move to make the defense move. If the opposition plays the ball instead of their assigned men, a constant barrage of quick, sharp passes will soon have them back on their heels.

To keep your team in top shape, you may use any conditioning program that is recommended for full court basketball, but emphasize those phases of the program that are addressed to stop-and-go movement and quick changes of direction.

Regardless of your preference in conditioning programs, the important thing is to *have* such a program. Casual three-on-three players are not accustomed to the repetitious rigors of training, but Halfcourt® basketball is a competitive sport and requires this kind of dedication. Don't forget, under Halfcourt® rules, only the Official may call time-out, so you can't give your players a breather whenever you think they need it.

Robert Martin (Bob) Smalt, varsity basketball coach at the New York Military Academy, is experienced in both full court and Halfcourt® basketball and has formulated the following pregame warm-up program specifically for Halfcourt®.

1. Stretching
   a. 20 alternate toe touches.
   b. 10 deep knee bends.
   c. Take hold of both ankles for a ten-second period to loosen the lower back and the hamstring muscles.
   d. Hurdler stretch: Place right leg forward while in a sitting position; with left leg in a bent position, place your head to your right knee. (Hold this position for a five-second period, then repeat.)
   e. Hurdler stretch: Alternate with the left leg.
2. Exercises
   a. 10 jumping jacks.
   b. 10 sit-ups.
   c. 10 push-ups.
   d. 10 quick jumps (high into the air, staying on the toes).
3. Running
   3 laps around the court.

Two other exercises may be added:

1. A shooting warm-up, to give the players their scoring eye and to allow them to get the feel of the court.

2. A take-back exercise, which simulates the all-important transitional situation. One way to set this up (there are many) is to station one player in rebounding position under the board, a second in take-back position behind the free throw line, and a third floating from one shooting position to another. During the

exercise, the floating player shoots, and the rebounder takes the ball off the board and passes it to the player behind the free throw line, who then sets up the shooter again, in a new position. (See Fig. 3-1.)

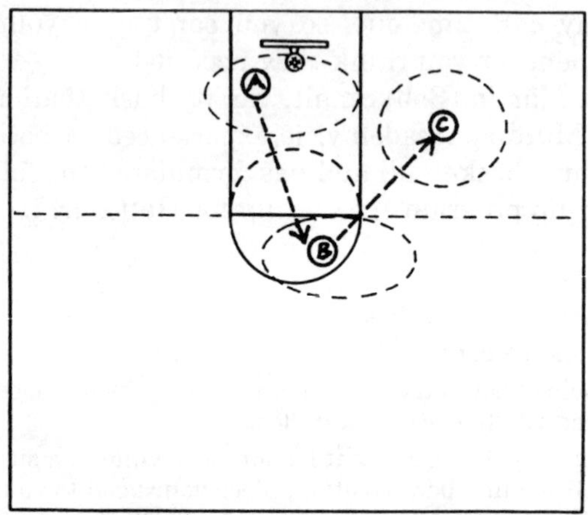

Figure 3-1. *Take-Back Exercise*—In this example of the take-back exercise, player C is the shooter, and his preferred shooting area is to the right of the free throw lane. Player B will move about in the area immediately in back of the take-back line and will "cheat" a little in the direction of C. Player A is the rebounder and will practice anticipating the direction of the rebound on any shot that C misses. All three players will concentrate on moving the ball quickly and on sensing their teammates movements in advance.

Bob Smalt believes that pregame warm-ups will reduce injuries and help get the players into a state of physical and mental readiness at the start of the game. The way a team starts a Halfcourt® game does a lot to determine the momentum of that game and its eventual outcome. From the physical standpoint, Bob believes that the greatest emphasis should be placed on the lower body, particularly the knee, ankle, thigh muscle, and calf muscle. "These are your wheels," he says.

He also points out that a lot of Halfcourt® is played on hard outdoor surfaces that require footwear with lots of cushion and all-around grip. "Your sneaker," he explains, "is part of your wheel, too."

PRACTICE SESSIONS

Any team entering an official Halfcourt® basketball tournament will have up to five players on its roster. If a coach wishes to hold a closed practice session, he can set up a three-on-three situation by participating himself, by recruiting a volunteer or assistant coach, or by carrying a sixth player who is not entered in the tournament. A closed practice session in Halfcourt® is almost as good as a game, because everybody gets to play and it is very easy to simulate Halfcourt® game conditions. Game-situation practice has several purposes. It incorporates your instructions on set plays and fundamentals into the flow of the game. The tendency among many players is to forget during the game the things they learned in drills. When this happens in game-situation practice, call a halt and run through the weak spot a few times.

Game practice also allows players to get to know each other. This is the key to teamwork. For example, it is important for each player to read every teammate's moves, to know when he is faking and when he is moving for real so that he can throw lead passes without throwing the ball away, to know when to hold his position for a block and when to clear out for a one-on-one move, and so on. There is ample evidence that playing together improves a Halfcourt® team's chances of winning.

Practice games help establish a tempo. The spirit and letter of Halfcourt® rules require constant offensive pressure. This is an area of judgment for the Official, who can issue a warning or impose a technical foul or other penalties for delay of game. Recreational three-on-three does not teach this, so practice sessions must. In practicing the game at a no-coasting pace, you will also be able to measure stamina and develop a mental index on how long to leave each player in the game. The same index will guide you on giving some players extra work on conditioning. Some of the signs of fatigue to look for are:

Holding hands low on defense.
Excessive fouling.
A tendency to be unaggressive.

Game-situation practice should be supplemented by one-on-one practice and individual instruction and evaluation. Some suggestions follow.

1. *Switching.* Simulate game situations that force players to switch on defense. Set up an offensive block, or have an offensive player "get past" his defender. Part of teaching to switch is training players to *call* for the switch when they are blocked or faked out of the play.

2. *Blocking out and following up* (a one-on-one drill). One player shoots and tries to follow his shot for the rebound. The second player tries to stop the shot, then block the shooter's path to the rebound.

3. *Rebounding* (a one-on-one drill). The coach or a player shoots the ball from various spots, allowing a few seconds before each shot for the two players in the exercise to maneuver for rebounding position. The purpose is to let each player learn the best way to use his body to gain position and to anticipate the direction of the rebound.

4. *Dribbling* (an individual or one-on-one drill). The goal is to teach how to move the ball while protecting it. Instruct the player to keep his body between the ball and the defender, to dribble close to the body, and to keep his head up while dribbling so he can see the rest of the court. Part of the discipline of Halfcourt® is to learn to dribble well, yet not to dribble too much. The rule is: The player moves fastest without the ball, and the ball moves fastest without the player.

5. *Take-back exercise.* This is described under "Conditioning" as a pregame warm-up. It is also an essential part of practice sessions.

6. *Evaluation.* Individual and one-on-one drills will provide your best opportunity to evaluate talent. Although you are training for versatility, you always want to go with your strength. You

want to have your best rebounders nearest the basket, your best ball handlers in control of the ball, and your best shooters shooting.

Study Chapter 2 to get a more complete idea of the kind of performance players should aspire to. This will suggest other drills that you can add to your training program. It's a good idea to vary your training sessions just for the sake of interest. Halfcourt® should never be boring.

SET PLAYS

Figs. 3-2 through 3-16 present diagrams of suggested set plays. Any movement from right to left can be reversed. This is an important option in setting up a play for a shooter who favors one hand. You will usually want him to shoot with his shooting hand away from the basket so that his body shields him from his defender.

Although many set plays show only two players involved in the action, the third player always has an important role. His responsibilities include keeping his defender away from the play in progress, positioning himself for a rebound, chasing a loose ball, moving into defensive position quickly if the ball changes hands, and calling for the ball if he finds himself free for a shot. He will also be able to spot defects in the other team's defense that can be exploited later.

Figure 3-2. Symbols.

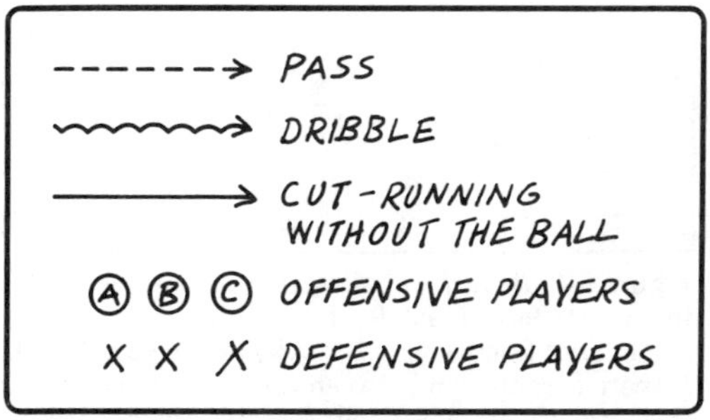

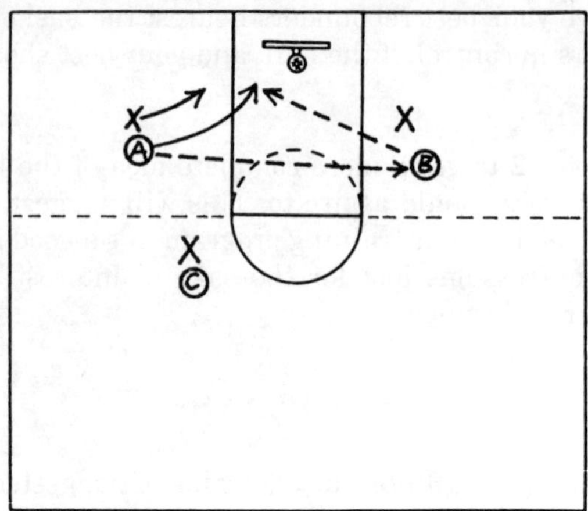

Figure 3-3. *Give and Go*—This is the most basic two-man play in basketball. Player A passes to B and cuts for the basket. If A's defender reacts slowly, A will be free for a return pass from B. If B's defender switches to pick up A, A passes back to B, who will be free for a shot. (The pass back to B is not shown in the diagram.)

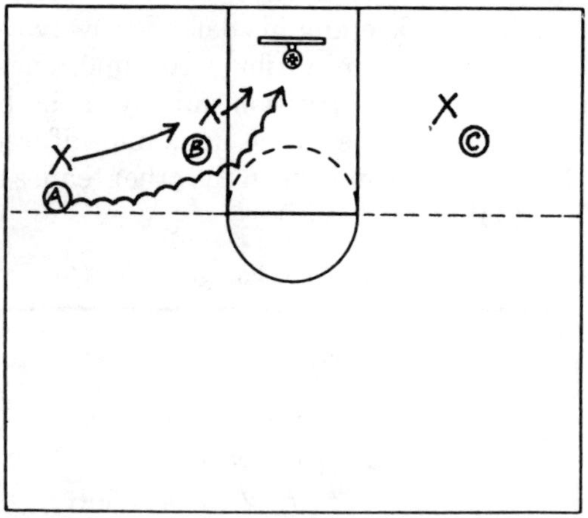

Figure 3-4. *Basic Pick*—Player A dribbles behind B in order to force his defender to collide with the defender of B or to force B's defender to switch to A. If there is confusion between the two defenders or if they are late on the switch, A maintains his dribble and continues to the basket for a shot.

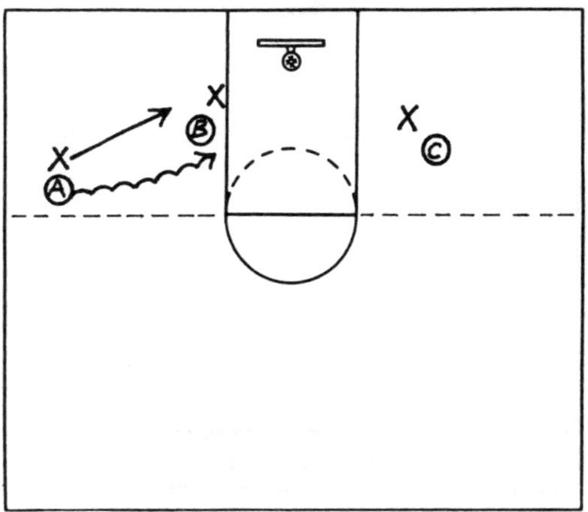

Figure 3-5. *Basic Screen*—The Basic Pick becomes a Screen if player A does not continue to the basket but stops behind player B, using him as a shield so that he can shoot. The Screen is effective when the defenders do not come out to meet A. This is called "fighting through the screen." The Pick or Screen can be worked with B passing the ball to A after A has moved into position behind B. When B has the ball with his back to the basket, he is in pivot position and had various other options, including the Pick and Roll.

Players should be trained to value possession over risky shooting. If a play is completed and the shooter finds himself closely defended or out of position, he should forego the shot, abandon the "broken" play, and start over.

GAME STRATEGY

How you direct your players in a game will depend largely on what is working best for your team that day and what kind of team you are playing. You should have an overall style and philosophy and work with the strengths of your personnel, but each game is a little different and presents special opportunities. Learn to take advantage of them.

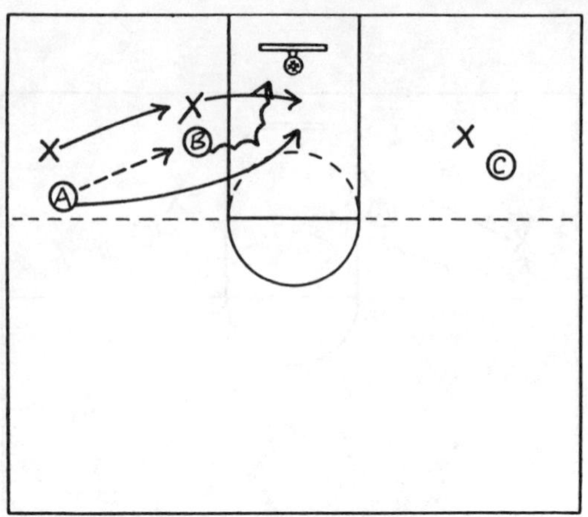

Figure 3-6. *Pick and Roll*—In this version of the Pick and Roll, player A passes the ball to B and moves toward him as in the Pick or Screen play. However B's defender comes out to meet A successfully on the switch. But before A's defender can position himself between B and the basket, B rolls toward the basket using a long step and lowered head and shoulder to gain inside position. Note that the path taken by B on the dribble can be slightly to one side of the basket in order to keep his defender away from the inside position and to make the other defender cover more distance if he tries to switch back to B.

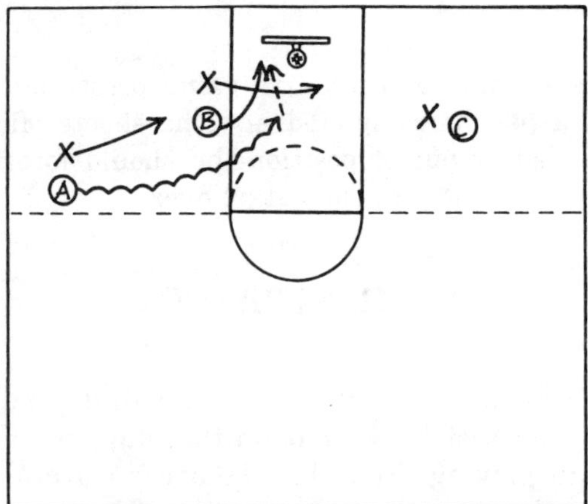

Figure 3-7. *Pick and Roll Variation*—This variation starts with player A dribbling the ball to force the defenders to switch. Player B then rolls to the basket and receives a pass from A.

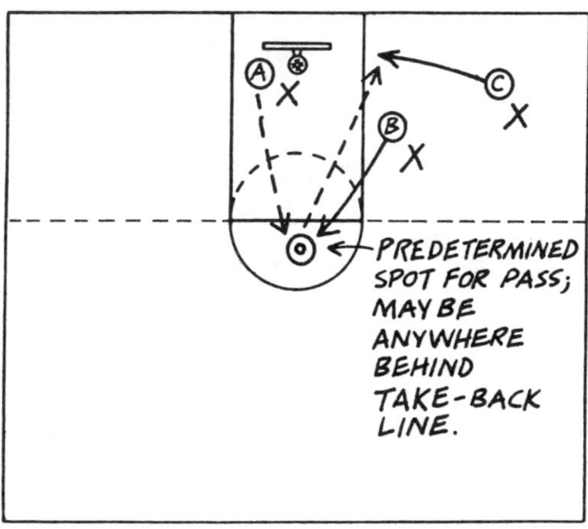

Figure 3-8. *Halfcourt® Fast Break*—A takes a defensive rebound (his team then becomes the offensive team). He calls the signal for a fast break and passes to a predetermined spot behind the take-back line. B, who is the nearest player to that spot, cuts behind the line to receive the pass and throws a quick pass to C who is cutting for the basket. C has to retain the inside position he had when he was on defense, so it takes quick automatic movements to make this play work.

If possible, scout the other team. Is there a poor ball handler who can give you some turnovers? Does the team look for one player to do all the scoring? Are team members slow in making the transition to defense? Learn their weaknesses and exploit them. Some of the weaknesses may be exposed during the course of the game. Learn to pick them out, and have your substitutes do the same. It will help them prepare mentally for their return to the floor, and they might spot something that you miss. If nothing else, it gives them an active role while they are not in the game.

During warm-ups, scout your own team. See who is "up" for the game. You want to start with eager, aggressive players. But don't place too much importance on how well anyone hits his shots in practice. Often a player who is hot before the game cools off later, and vice versa.

If you want to go with set plays, start with the ones your players are most familiar with. They can get into the flow of the game easier that way. Also, they can get the most mileage out of their best plays by using them early, switching to other strategies

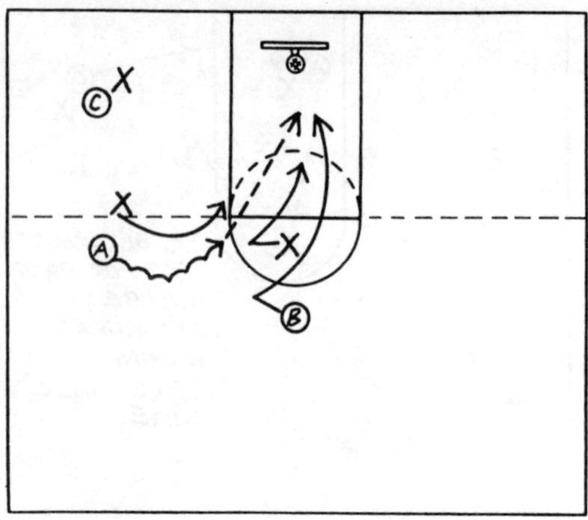

Figure 3-9. *Back Door*—B cuts toward A. His defender is tempted to overshift when he sees A dribbling toward him. B reverses direction and his defensemen is forced to turn his back on the ball in order to follow him. A then throws a lead pass to B. Bounce and lob passes are recommended for the Back Door play so that the ball does not pass B's defender at arm level where it may be intercepted. There are many Back Door variations. In all of them the ball is passed around the "wrong" side of the defender when his head is turned.

during the middle of the game, then coming back with their best at the end.

SUBSTITUTIONS

Substitutions are more important in Halfcourt® than in other major team sports. A substitute in football replaces one-eleventh of the team. A substitute in full court basketball replaces one-fifth of the team. A Halfcourt® substitute replaces one-third of the team. Therefore, each substitution must be carefully considered.

Consider the player coming off the court. Why are you pulling him? Is he tired? Is he messing up plays? Is he giving up too many points? On the other hand, is he pressing too hard because he's afraid of being yanked? Maybe you go a little longer with some players to give them confidence. When you do that, it is helpful to tell the player what's happening. He may need to know that you are not overcritical or "out to get" him.

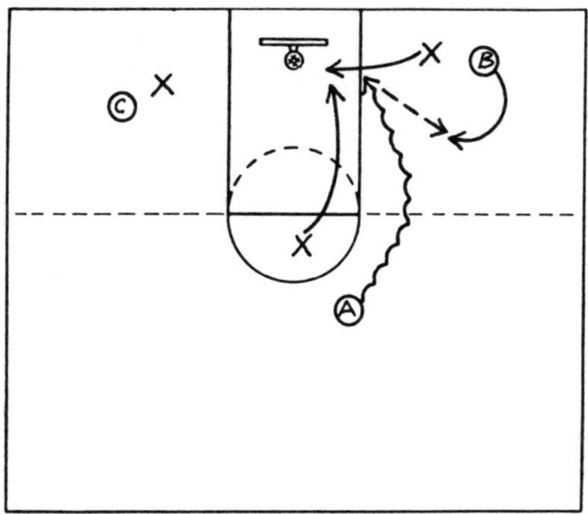

Figure 3-10. *Rick Barry Special, Part One*—This play combines the talents of a penetrating scorer and a player with an "automatic" outside shot, like Rick Barry and Calvin Murphy who worked it to perfection. Player A (Barry) drives to the hoop in a way that intentionally draws off the defender of B (Murphy) on a switch. B moves to his shooting spot, and A flips the ball back to him.

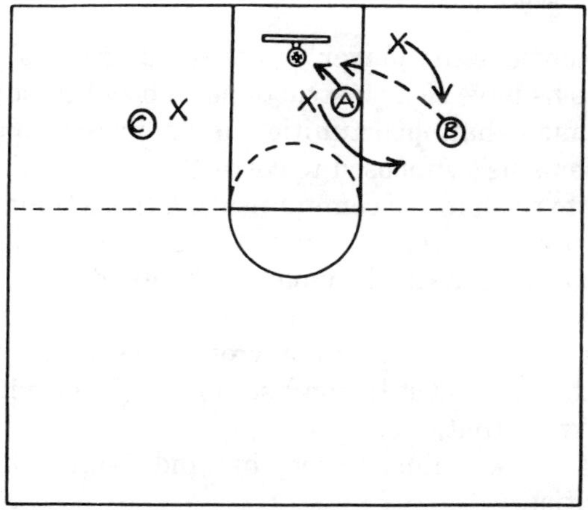

Figure 3-11. *Rick Barry Special, Part Two*—If the defenders of A and B overreact and both follow the ball to B, player A will be left open for an easy layup. B is required to be unselfish and pass off even when he is in his favorite spot, and A must keep moving to the hoop and be mentally pass-receptive.

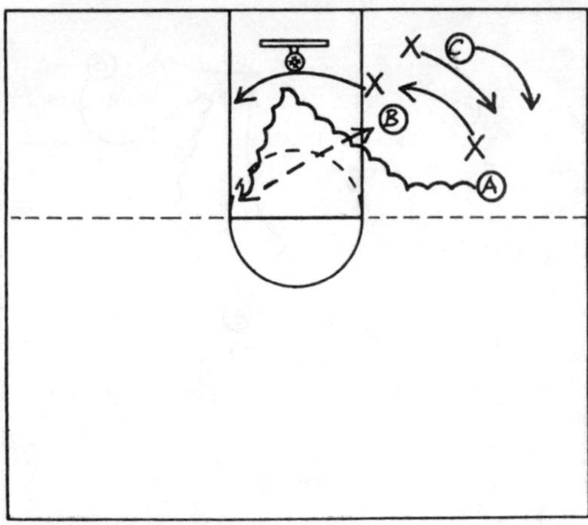

Figure 3-12. *Forcing a Switch, Clearing Out*—This is one of many ways to create a height advantage and capitalize on it. In the situation diagrammed, player B is taller than A's defender so A dribbles past B to force the defenders to switch, leaving A to be covered by the short man. Player A continues his dribble away from the basket to draw his defender away from player B before passing to B. Player C also draws his defender away, thus clearing out the area around the basket for B to go one-on-one against the short man.

Now consider the player you're sending in. Is he mentally ready? Does he have clear instructions on how he's supposed to fit into the game, what opportunities he's supposed to exploit, and what problems he's supposed to correct?

Get into the habit of communicating these things constantly with your bench players, because there's very little time to go over all your thoughts at the moment of substitution. And when a player comes off the court, tell him why you took him out of the game. If he was doing something wrong, he should know in order to correct it. If the substitution had nothing to do with mistakes, he should know that, too.

There are two things to keep in mind about Halfcourt® rules on substitution:

1. You may substitute any time the ball is dead.
2. When one team makes a substitution, the other team must be given an opportunity to make an equal substitution.

This makes substituting a real duel of wits between coaches. Once you commit yourself on a substitution, you may not have an opportunity to change your mind until a basket is scored, and that could be critical. Also, the other coaches' substitution will raise many questions and possibilities, and you have to keep from over-responding. By substituting simply to counter the other coach's move, you may be breaking up a good combination.

Substitutions make the role of the coach extremely important and give a well-coached team an advantage over a poorly coached or uncoached team. A pro basketball coach once remarked that he loved going against inexperienced coaches and that against a rookie coach he was worth a few points a game. The same can be said for Halfcourt®.

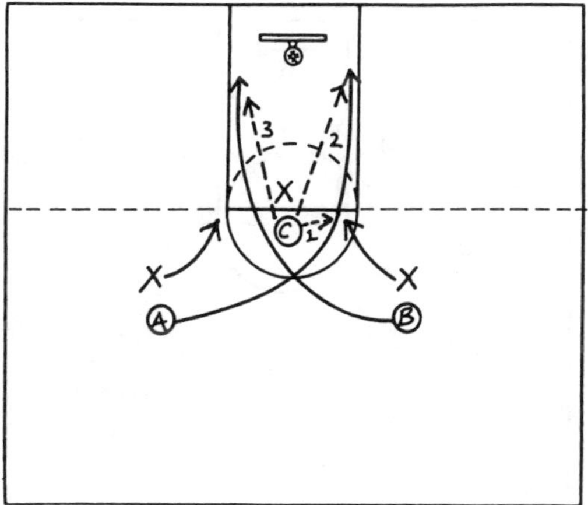

Figure 3-13. *Double Pick or Scissors*—Players A and B cut around C, who is in pivot, or post, position and is holding the ball. In the congestion A or B may lose his defender and can receive a pass that will lead to a layup or jump shot. The diagram shows three passing options for C. Option 1 is a classic hand-off to A. Since this is the pass the defenders will probably be expecting, C has the option to fake the hand-off and allow A to continue past his defender without the ball. C will then throw pass 2, which should be a lob pass thrown with a hook motion. Pass 3 is a similar lob pass thrown to player B, who may be free if his defender thinks he is out of the play.

DEALING WITH THE OFFICIAL

In Halfcourt® competition, a single Official usually handles officiating, scorekeeping, and timekeeping. The combination is not burdensome, but it can become so if players and coaches create distractions. Full cooperation with the Official will do more to influence him favorably toward you than arguing, if that is part of your thinking, and it will certainly make the game more enjoyable for everyone involved.

By reading the Halfcourt® rules carefully, as well as Chapter 5 of this book, you'll get a good idea of how the Official wants the game to go, what will help him, and what will hinder him. Following are some key points to remember in this respect.

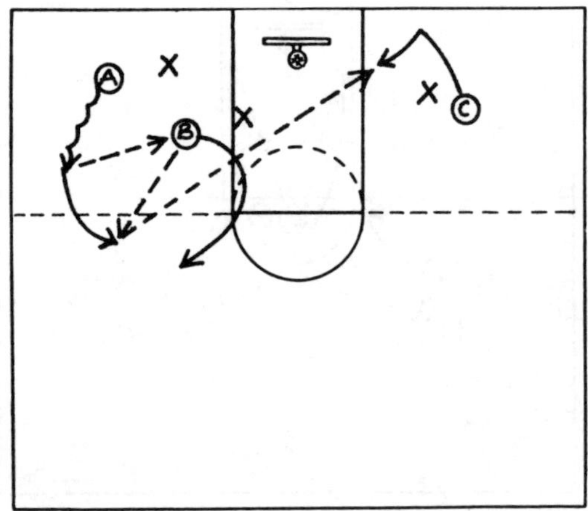

Figure 3-14. *Weak Side Sleeper*—Any sleeper play makes use of a player who appears to be outside of the action. He is the "sleeper." In the diagrammed example players A and B execute various passing, cutting, and dribbling maneuvers, waiting for C's defender to relax or look away. Then C maneuvers into shooting position and receives a pass from whichever of his two teammates has the ball. Sleeper plays are not always planned but can often arise as opportunity plays during the normal course of a game. Note: The diagrammed play is called a weak side play because it involves a player who is on the side of the court away from the ball, the "weak" side.

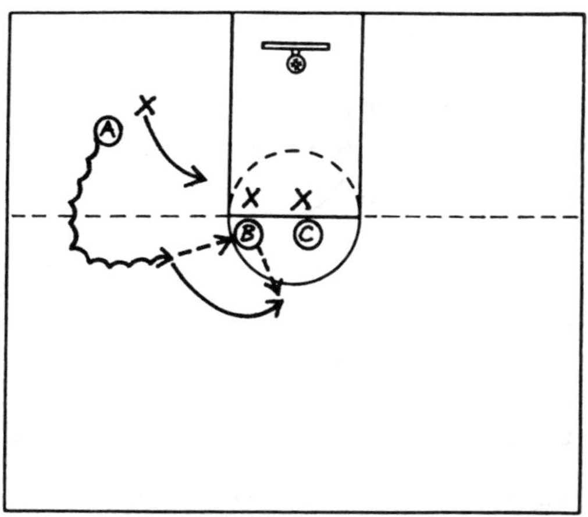

Figure 3-15. *Double Screen*—This play offers player A many options. At the completion of the action diagrammed he can shoot, dribble left or right, or pass to players B or C if they roll to the basket. A lot depends upon the reaction of A's defender. Since A has the ball and the best view of the action, he should be the one to signal for B or C to roll to the hoop. One surprise option is for A to dribble straight down the middle between B and C, since each of the two defenders in the free throw lane may be depending upon the other to protect the middle. The Double Screen is not a single play but the basis for several plays involving all three players.

Halfcourt® is supposed to be hassle-free, just like the playground game out of which it grew. The rules make fouling unprofitable, and calling fouls on the team instead of the individual also helps avoid confrontations. You can do your share by coaching in the same spirit. Give the Official any information he asks for before, during, or after the game. If he needs assistance, like correcting a bent rim, volunteer to help him. If you're unhappy about a call and you *must* vent your feelings, do it as mildly as possible, and pick a time when he's not concentrating on the game.

Maintaining offensive pressure is a *judgment* call. If the Official says your players are stalling, the burden is on your team and not on the Official. When he issues a warning, get the talk going among your players, or even send in an eager sub, if that

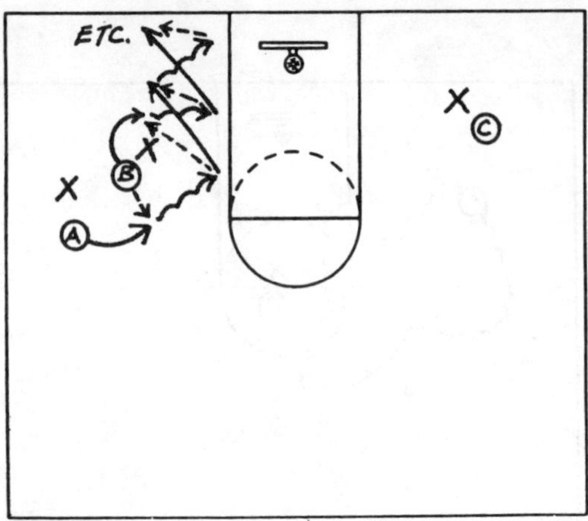

Figure 3-16. *Two-Man Grinder*—In this play, two players take turns dribbling, passing off, and cutting for a return pass, performing crisscross patterns and forcing the defenders to switch and change directions constantly. Any lapse by a defender creates the opportunity for a shot. To make the diagram easier to read, follow the movements of one player all the way through. For example, if you are player A, you cut and receive a pass from B, then dribble briefly, and pass back to B, who has moved to a new position closer to the basket. As B dribbles, you cut behind him and receive a return pass. The play may continue as diagrammed, or you may find yourself open for a shot.

makes sense. If you argue the warning, that will only confirm the Official's opinion that you are trying to delay the game.

Toward the end of the game, if a situation arises that causes a delay that is unfair to one team, the Official is empowered to correct the inequity by stopping the clock or imposing penalties. A good Official will see to it that delaying tactics backfire, so don't think of loopholes, think of the rules, and think in the Halfcourt® spirit.

TRAINING BEGINNERS

Halfcourt® is an excellent way for youngsters to enter the world of basketball, to develop the skills they will need to move on to full court, and to get early experience in the continuation sport that Halfcourt® is. These are some of the advantages of Halfcourt® for beginners:

1. It doesn't turn into a footrace, as full court often does.
2. It allows the coach to instruct the players during a game without following them up and down the court.
3. Single baskets are much more available than full two-basket courts.
4. Six players on the court instead of ten reduces the confusion and permits more visibility and freedom of movement.
5. Halfcourt® takes the emphasis off dribbling, which is the most difficult skill for learning players.

For training purposes, the coach should consider some developmental variations of Halfcourt®. One coach tells about getting beginners started by stationing them on the sidelines as "passers." They put the ball in play and receive and throw passes while the game is in progress. In addition to learning passing skills, they become familiar with basketball movement and strategy. Then, after individual training in other fundamentals, they can move onto the court.

Other modifications can be made for developmental purposes:*

Employ an eight-foot basket (for very young players).
Omit the three-second rule.
Make inbound passes "free" (no interceptions allowed).
Allow the coaches to call time-outs.
Shorten the playing time; reduce the point total.

These variations and others you may know about come right out of playground three-on-three. They have helped millions of players train for basketball and can serve the same purpose in your program.

THE FULL COURT CONNECTION

If you are working with a full court basketball program, Halfcourt® can be a worthwhile addition to it. Here are some ways that the two games can complement each other:

*For programs involving mentally retarded players, see the rules developed by HBI for Special Olympics at the end of Chapter 6.

- Players who are cut from the full court program compete in a Halfcourt® league.
- Players from the two top Halfcourt® teams in a tournament are combined into one full court team for a second tournament.
- Players who are waiting their turn for full court scrimmage play Halfcourt® on side baskets.
- Before or after practice, the full court roster is broken down into a Halfcourt® league to develop versatility. The personnel is switched around at intervals to experiment with different combinations.
- Halfcourt® is used in the early phases of tryouts for the full court team. Strengths and weaknesses show up quickly, all the players get into the action, and it's easy viewing for the coach.

BOYS AND GIRLS TOGETHER

There is a trend to mixed male-female competition in sports that must be accommodated by schools, municipalities, and other agencies that serve the public. As administrators become more familiar with Halfcourt® basketball, they discover that the game is ideal for mixed competition, and coaches will be handling an ever increasing number of such programs. Coaching mixed Halfcourt® is almost the same as all-male or all-female Halfcourt®, with one key exception: The five players on the roster must include at least two females, and there must be at least one female on the court at all times.

As a result, the coach has to deal with two rotations of substitution. For the males, he will have one on the bench to replace either of two on the court, and for the females it will be a straight one-for-one. This limits his strategic options, but it does suggest one new strategy: Work out male-female pairs that have special combined abilities and bring them into the game that way.

One pair may be especially adept at high-pressure defense and ball stealing. Another may be strong in rebounding and transition. The effect of a sudden two-thirds change of personnel and a shift in the style of the game could have a shock effect on the other team. Also, if the pairs have worked on a programmed series of plays, they can turn to that repertoire toward the end of a close game. The strategy is similar to the two-minute drill in football.

It should be noted that there is no rule against having more than two females on the roster or more than one on the court. One of the problems in mixed competition is contact. Full court basketball started out as a no-contact sport, but it has evolved into a modified version of the original, which could be called "controlled contact" or "collision" or some other compromise term. Halfcourt®, by virtue of its nature and rules, is less of a contact sport than full court. The straightaway footrace down the full length of the court that results in high-speed collisions and spills does not exist in Halfcourt®. Furthermore, Halfcourt® has a rule that forbids hand checking, and Officials are instructed not to cut corners in enforcing it. The rule is especially appropriate for mixed competition, but it was not inspired by mixed competition. It is completely in the spirit of Halfcourt®.

4

The Program Director's Guide to Halfcourt® Basketball

WESTCHESTER

Halfcourt® basketball is an ideal addition to any program of organized sports. It makes maximum use of facilities and personnel and addresses a broad cross section of the population—male and female, preteen through middle age. Anyone with basic basketball skills can play Halfcourt®, yet even a pro can find it challenging. And while conditioning is an advantage, the strength and stamina required by Halfcourt® are well within the capacity of the part-time athlete. Last but not least, the game is fun. For all these reasons, Halfcourt® basketball has been adopted by institutions everywhere that provide recreational services, including schools, colleges, Y branches, summer camps, and municipal recreation departments.

Organizations that have basic athletic facilities, equipment, and staff will not require special funding for Halfcourt® basketball. In fact, Halfcourt® has been used by some institutions to save money (by replacing a more expensive activity) or to raise funds (through sign-up fees, sponsorship, or admission charges). HBI can provide organizations with individual guidance on the financial aspects of Halfcourt®.

SCHEDULING: THE GAME UNITS SYSTEM

The easiest way to schedule a Halfcourt® program is to calculate in terms of game units. Your game units equal the number of courts (one basket, with properly marked floor) multiplied by the

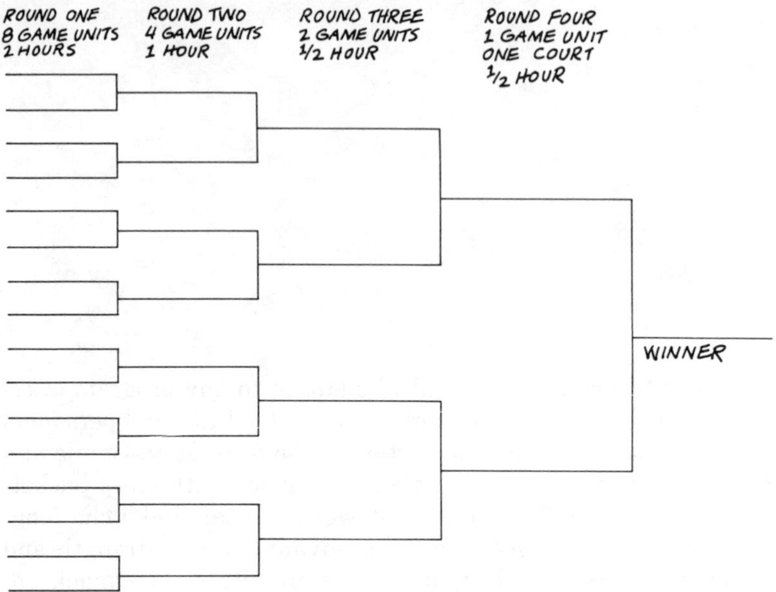

Figure 4-1. 16-team single elimination using two baskets—total playing time is 4 hours.

number of half hours (thirty minutes per game) that the courts are available. If, for example, you have a gymnasium with four baskets, and the gym is available to you for five hours (ten half hours) on a given day, you have forty game units for that day, minus any units lost for lunch breaks and other downtime.

Within those forty units you can schedule an eight-team round robin (twenty-eight games), which will give each team seven games with three half-hour breaks. In this example, forty players (eight teams with five players per roster) enjoy a complete and exciting basketball program in one day. The following formulas are provided to help the program director calculate the maximum number of games that can be played with a given number of teams, baskets, and playing hours.

1. *Round robin* (each team plays every other team once). Multiply the number of teams by one less than the number of teams,

then divide by two. For example, in an eight-team round robin, figure 8 × 7 = 56, then 56 ÷ 2 = 28.

2. *Single elimination*. (One loss eliminates the team see Fig. 4-1.) The number of games played equals the number of teams minus one. For example, in a 200-team single elimination, the number of games played is 199.

3. *Double elimination, triple elimination, and so on.* Multiply the number of teams by the number of games it takes to eliminate a team. For example, a double-elimination program with thirty teams will require approximately sixty games, and a triple elimination with ten teams will require approximately thirty games. These figures are approximate because one team (the winner) will lose *at least* one game less than the other teams. The total number of games will also vary according to any variation in the formula that is used for play-offs. For example, in a single elimination, the final four teams may switch to double elimination, which is often referred to as "best two of three," or the two finalists may play a triple elimination, or "best three of five." (See Fig. 4-2.)

Figure 4-2. 8-team double elimination using two baskets—total playing time is 4 to 4½ hours. If the winner of game 13 wins game 14, they each have one loss and it is necessary to play game 15 (half hour, one court) to determine a winner.

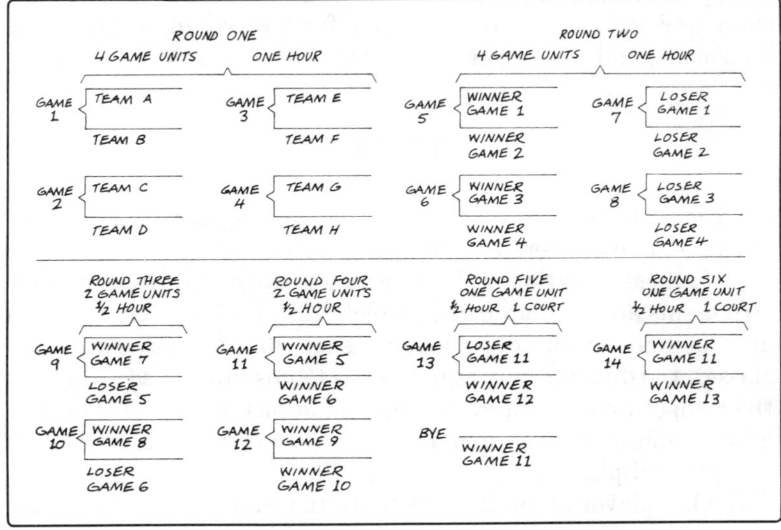

Whatever schedule you select, plan it out on a draw sheet and fill in the team names at the beginning and after each round. Keep a copy of the draw sheet posted so that participants and interested parties can keep track of the competition.

In any round of competition that includes an odd number of teams, you will have to give one team a bye, or free pass, to the next round. The bye can be awarded by a flip of the coin, a free throw contest, or any other equitable method, but make sure that the same team does not receive more than one bye, and get rid of all your byes in the early rounds, so that one team does not skip a round when the going is toughest. Your best situation for fair scheduling is a grouping of sixteen, eight, or four teams going into the late rounds.

If it is not necessary to set your schedule before sign-ups, you can select your format after you know how many teams are in the program, then divide the number of game units by the number of teams. The figure you get will suggest a playing format. For example, if you have eighty game units and forty teams or thereabouts, you can plan on a double-elimination tournament.

For a complete time frame, add advance time for sign-ups, staff training, dissemination of information (to parents, media, etc.), preparation of printed material, and ordering of uniforms, then add post-tournament time for award presentations, luncheons, and other special events.

TEAMS

Halfcourt® basketball is played by two teams, each with a roster of five—three starters and two substitutes.

In most situations it is advisable to have players form their own teams and sign up with complete rosters of five. However, in development-oriented programs, such as physical education classes, the director may organize the teams himself so as to keep the competition balanced. He may hand-pick each roster or may allow teams of three to sign up and then add two more players out of a general players' pool.

One player on each team is elected captain and (in the absence of a coach) is responsible for substitutions, providing required information to Officials, informing players about schedules and locations, and meeting other league obligations.

Here are two ways to vary your schedule and sign-up procedure. Award points for the top teams each week, then have a play-off at the end of the program for the two or four teams with the most points. This makes each week a championship season, yet gives continuity and incentive to the overall schedule. You also can hold one-day drop-in tournaments. These can be used to familiarize players with your organization and encourage membership. They also can serve as training programs for Halfcourt® players before they enter larger tournaments. Open sign-ups are appropriate for drop-in tournaments—each player signs up individually and is assigned to a team at random.

For guidance in the structuring of leagues (by age, height, etc.), refer to Chapter 6 of this book.

OFFICIALS

Anyone with a good understanding of basketball can become a Halfcourt® Official quickly, but whether or not he is experienced in officiating, he *must* study the rules, as there are major differences between full court and Halfcourt®. Since experience is the best teacher, it is advisable to assign Officials in training to work practice games. In these sessions the players and Officials become accustomed to officiated three-on-three together.

A Halfcourt® game requires only one Official, who also serves as Scorekeeper and Timekeeper. In the foregoing example (a five-hour program in a four-basket gym), four Officials can handle the entire tournament in an eight-hour day, with sufficient time left over for pre- and post-tournament briefing, paperwork, and other details. If more than one Official per basket is available, duties may be divided as specified in the rules.

Halfcourt® officiating is a good internship opportunity for college phys. ed. majors, and interns are a good source of competent Officials for community Halfcourt® programs. In schools, sports camps, and other institutions where leadership training is part of the curriculum, the players in a Halfcourt® program can be trained to double as Officials. When player-Officials are used, it is recommended that there be two Officials per game, each from a different team and neither from a team participating in the game.

UNIFORMS

Halfcourt® programs may be outfitted as follows:

1. Standard basketball uniforms, each team in a different color.

Figure 4-3. Two intramural Halfcourt® basketball players and an official at Salisbury State College, Salisbury, Md., receive instructions from Grady Armstrong, Intramural Director. The players are outfitted in official Halfcourt® T-shirts, the light color designating the "home" team and the dark color, the "visiting" team.

2. Two sets of standard basketball uniforms, one in a light color (for home games) and one in a dark color (for away).

3. Two T-shirts for each player, with the same two colors used for every player in the program (see Fig. 4-3). When any two teams meet, one is designated the home team and wears the light shirt, and the other is designated the away team and wears the dark shirt (like playground skins and shirts). Under this system, you simply order a quantity of shirts in each color equal to the total number of players. Size information is provided by players on the sign-up form (see Fig. 4-4). If it is necessary to order shirts before the size information is available, consult with your supplier as to the size scale (percentage of small, medium, large, etc.) that is standard for the particular age and gender of *your* player group. When in doubt, take the next *larger* size. A player can move around in a shirt that is loose but not in one that is

Figure 4-4. Sign-up form can be printed as a post card by using post-card stock and printing return address on reverse. Also indicate place for a stamp and amount of postage. Oversized cards require First Class postage. (Check Post Office for size limits.) Note: Spaces for shirt size, jacket size, etc., as shown above, are used only if these items are provided by the tournament.

This area used for:

Name of tournament.

Sign-up instructions, including mailing address, deadline date, limitations by age, gender, etc.

Special requirements, such as proof of age, dress code, medical examination, etc.

Fees, if any.

Check-off spaces for preferred playing site or division.

Release of claims.

Names of sponsors and host organization.

Note referring to minimum of three players per roster.

CAPTAIN

1. PRINT NAME SIGNATURE
STREET ADDRESS (INCLUDE APT. NO.)
CITY STATE ZIP
PHONE CHECK SHIRT SIZE M☐ L☐ XL☐
CHECK JACKET SIZE S☐ M☐ L☐ XL☐

2. PRINT NAME SIGNATURE
STREET ADDRESS (INCLUDE APT. NO.)
CITY STATE ZIP
PHONE CHECK SHIRT SIZE M☐ L☐ XL☐
CHECK JACKET SIZE S☐ M☐ L☐ XL☐

3. PRINT NAME SIGNATURE
STREET ADDRESS (INCLUDE APT. NO.)
CITY STATE ZIP
PHONE CHECK SHIRT SIZE M☐ L☐ XL☐
CHECK JACKET SIZE S☐ M☐ L☐ XL☐

4. PRINT NAME SIGNATURE
STREET ADDRESS (INCLUDE APT. NO.)
CITY STATE ZIP
PHONE CHECK SHIRT SIZE M☐ L☐ XL☐
CHECK JACKET SIZE S☐ M☐ L☐ XL☐

5. PRINT NAME SIGNATURE
STREET ADDRESS (INCLUDE APT. NO.)
CITY STATE ZIP
PHONE CHECK SHIRT SIZE M☐ L☐ XL☐
CHECK JACKET SIZE S☐ M☐ L☐ XL☐

tight. When ordering shirts, allow time for any screen printing that has to be done. (Official Halfcourt® T-shirts are available through HBI.)

4. Reversible shirts. The two sides of a reversible shirt can be used in the same way as two contrasting T-shirts—light side for home team, dark side for away.

Officials are required to wear uniforms that are distinct from the players' uniforms. The black-and-white striped "zebra" shirt is preferred.

Figure 4-5. Blank official scorecard.

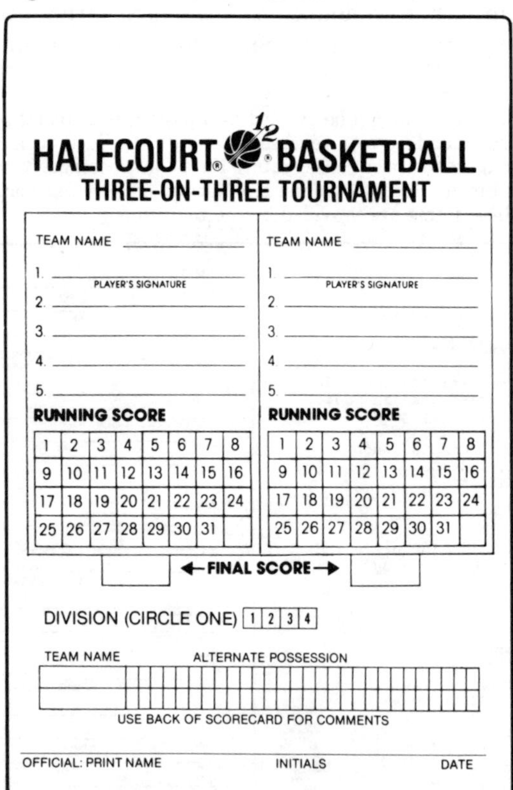

HALFCOURT® ½ BASKETBALL
THREE-ON-THREE TOURNAMENT

TEAM NAME ____________
1. ____________ PLAYER'S SIGNATURE
2. ____________
3. ____________
4. ____________
5. ____________

RUNNING SCORE

1	2	3	4	5	6	7	8
9	10	11	12	13	14	15	16
17	18	19	20	21	22	23	24
25	26	27	28	29	30	31	

TEAM NAME ____________
1. ____________ PLAYER'S SIGNATURE
2. ____________
3. ____________
4. ____________
5. ____________

RUNNING SCORE

1	2	3	4	5	6	7	8
9	10	11	12	13	14	15	16
17	18	19	20	21	22	23	24
25	26	27	28	29	30	31	

← FINAL SCORE →

DIVISION (CIRCLE ONE) 1 2 3 4

TEAM NAME ALTERNATE POSSESSION

USE BACK OF SCORECARD FOR COMMENTS

OFFICIAL: PRINT NAME INITIALS DATE

PRINTED MATERIALS

HBI has prepared official printed material, which it supplies to Halfcourt® programs. These items appear in this book for informational purposes. They are copyrighted and may not be reproduced.

1. Official sign-up form (Fig. 4-4). Can be distributed loose or in pads. If it is to be returned by mail, the form is printed as a postcard, with the return address on the reverse.
2. Official scorecard (Figs. 4-5 and 4-6).

Figure 4-6. Sample completed scorecard (check indicates starting player).

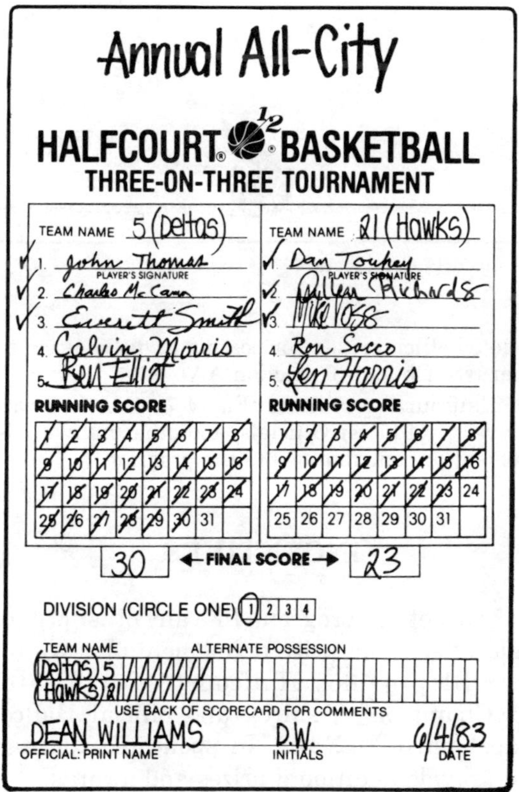

Annual All-City

HALFCOURT® ½ BASKETBALL

THREE-ON-THREE TOURNAMENT

TEAM NAME 5 (Deltas)	TEAM NAME 21 (Hawks)
✓ 1. John Thomas (PLAYER'S SIGNATURE)	✓ 1. Dan Touhey (PLAYER'S SIGNATURE)
✓ 2. Charles McCann	✓ 2. William Richards
✓ 3. Everett Smith	✓ 3. Mike Voss
4. Calvin Morris	4. Ron Sacco
5. Ben Elliot	5. Len Harris

RUNNING SCORE

1	2	3	4	5	6	7	8
9	10	11	12	13	14	15	16
17	18	19	20	21	22	23	24
25	26	27	28	29	30	31	

RUNNING SCORE

1	2	3	4	5	6	7	8
9	10	11	12	13	14	15	16
17	18	19	20	21	22	23	24
25	26	27	28	29	30	31	

30 ← FINAL SCORE → 23

DIVISION (CIRCLE ONE) 1 2 3 4

TEAM NAME ALTERNATE POSSESSION

(Deltas) 5

(Hawks) 21

USE BACK OF SCORECARD FOR COMMENTS

DEAN WILLIAMS — OFFICIAL: PRINT NAME

D.W. — INITIALS

6/4/83 — DATE

Figure 4-7. Halfcourt® Certificate.

3. Abbreviated official rules, for posting or distribution to each team or player (see Chapter 6, Section AA).
4. Official Halfcourt® certificate (Fig. 4-7). Can be awarded to winning players, volunteer Officials, and other individuals for special achievement or contributions to the program.

INCENTIVES

A Halfcourt® basketball program, like any other organized sports event, should offer some prize or memento for winning or participating. HBI provides Halfcourt® Certificates, special "Halfcourt® Champion" T-shirts, and official Halfcourt® gold-and-blue lapel pins (Fig. 4-8). In sponsored tournaments, the sponsor will provide additional prizes and awards.

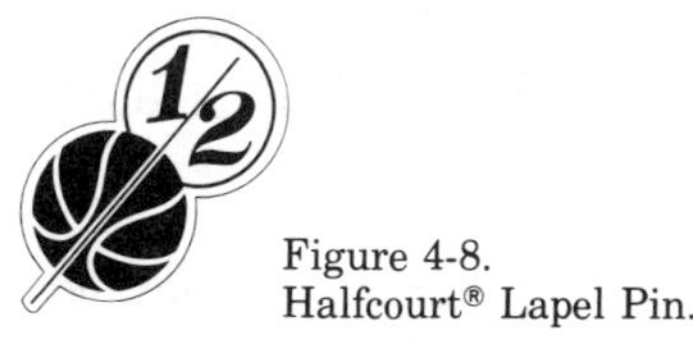

Figure 4-8.
Halfcourt® Lapel Pin.

STAFF

In addition to Officials, the Halfcourt® program director will need personnel to handle such administrative responsibilities as distribution and processing of sign-up forms, ordering and distribution of uniforms, issuing of equipment, distribution of printed materials, press contacts, bookkeeping, and record keeping. Some of these duties can be handled on a volunteer basis by players in the program, and most can be handled by the regular personnel of the host organization. It is important to remember that Halfcourt® is less demanding of detail work than most sports events; Halfcourt® action takes place on the court, not in the office.

COACHES

Coaches are an important asset to Halfcourt®. They provide the same benefits that coaches bring to any sports program, plus some others. Three-on-three players who have not participated in organized Halfcourt® competition are not accustomed to using set plays and planned strategies of offense or defense. A coach can instruct them in these areas and direct them during the game. He can run drills, practice sessions, and conditioning programs and can train individual players in adapting their basketball skills to the special requirements of Halfcourt®.

More important, coaches are symbolic of a sport's organized status. A Halfcourt® coach will give his players a sense of equality with players in other sports programs and provide youngsters with the early training needed to start them on a lifetime of good Halfcourt® habits.

SHARING THE HALFCOURT® EXPERIENCE

Because the director must understand the role of every participant in his Halfcourt® program—player, coach, Official—it is important for him to review the sections of this book that apply to those individuals. It is equally important for him to understand the full range of Halfcourt® adaptability, how it can accommodate the simplest little one-basket program for a group of friends as well as a citywide tournament for thousands of players.

The creative administrator will find ways to make Halfcourt® work even better. The opportunities are endless and within easy reach, and realizing them is a cooperative effort. Every Halfcourt® basketball program director is invited to become part of the network of administrators who share problems, ideas, and information through HBI.

PROGRAM TIPS

Following are some suggestions to get more excitement and greater rewards from your Halfcourt® basketball activities.

Special Events

Your organization can be represented in areawide events by a Halfcourt® basketball championship game, an all-star game, a demonstration, or a clinic. For example, the championship game of your organization's Halfcourt® tournament can be presented as a pregame attraction before a local high school or college full court game. Or it can be one of many events on a day of community pride, as it has been in Washington, D.C. on Recreation Day and in New York on Harlem Day.

Using Marginal Facilities

In most areas there are many basketball courts that go unused because one basket is broken or because of other obstacles to full court games. You can make these facilities productive with Halfcourt® programs.

Beginners' Tournaments

"Training Beginners" in Chapter 3 gives modifications of Halfcourt® basketball that can be employed to introduce young, unskilled, or handicapped players to the game. These modifications can be used to set up entire programs, so that players who are usually ignored can have a rewarding organized sports experience within the range of their abilities.

Home and Away

Add a "big time" dimension to your tournament by having the winners of your program play the winners from another area or organization. Even an informal event with a handful of spectators is meaningful to players who have not had the traveling experience that comes with organized sports.

Celebrity Appearances

Professional athletes, mayors, and other celebrities have accepted invitations to throw out the first ball, award prizes, and participate in various other ways in Halfcourt® programs. They respond because of their own personal lifelong identification with three-on-three. Extend invitations to your own local celebrities and make your program more exciting for everyone.

5

The Official's Guide to Halfcourt® Basketball

The most important step in transforming pickup three-on-three basketball into organized Halfcourt® was the introduction of the Official. The presence of the Official guarantees fair competition; gives credibility to every Halfcourt® league and tournament; certifies that honors, trophies, and prizes are honestly won; establishes uniform playing conditions, so that a team can travel anywhere with the assurance of competing on equal and familiar terms; and makes the game orderly and comprehensible for spectators.

To a great extent, the structure of Halfcourt® basketball as it exists today is the creation of working officials, and for that reason the sport gets high ratings when viewed from the standpoint of the arbiter—it is a smooth-running affair that requires little intervention and generates almost no arguing. The rules that appear in this book combine the original rules (published in 1977) with revisions based on thousands of supervised games. A number of the revisions were suggested by Officials like Earl Davis, a member of International Association of Approved Basketball Officials, who was head Official at HBI's first citywide tournament, in Anchorage, Alaska.

Davis worked the tournament with three other IAABO members—Jim Ridley, Dick Ames, and John Jones—and after it was over he called Halfcourt® basketball "an official's dream." He also described some of the ways in which he and his associates modified the rules as they stood at the time. "Instead of calling fouls on individual players," he said, "we just blew the whistle and hollered 'penalty,' then pointed to the player fouled and said,

'You're shooting.' No one ever questioned who committed the foul. That was a big reason why it went so smoothly, no chatter from the players.

"Normally I say, 'Nineteen blue, you're holding.' I'm setting up the start of a discussion. He sees me going to the table to signal and he's upset. The other way there's nothing said to the guy who committed the foul, and therefore there's no flak.

"A big problem in regular basketball develops when a player pushes or bumps his man from moving. Even if it has no effect you call it. We went by the principle of 'no harm, no foul.' That reduced the number of unnecessary interruptions immensely. The 'penalty' call is from international rules, and so is 'no harm, no foul.'

"Under a system of two shots and possession, there's no advantage to fouling. On a successful field goal we award one free throw, on a missed field goal we award two. You keep possession if you make or miss the free throw.

"Throughout the tournament we used just one Official, stationed under the basket. For the finals a second Official stationed along the halfcourt line took the pressure off . . . but it's not a necessity. A decent Official can handle Halfcourt® alone."

Because one Official *can* handle Halfcourt® alone, and since many host organizations (recreation departments, Ys, schools, and others) have limited staffs, Halfcourt® is organized so that one individual does all the officiating, scorekeeping, and timekeeping, with the option of delegating certain duties to other qualified people (see rules) when they are available. This system has two advantages. It allows for great flexibility in the use of personnel. At the beginning of a tournament, eight Officials can be spread out to work one basket each, handling a game every half hour. In the quarter-finals, semis, and finals, the same eight can be regrouped into teams of two and four for a full dress presentation that provides extra control. And every Official can keep working right through the schedule. It also allows for good on-court training. While the Official is handling major responsibilities from the end line, a Referee (the junior official) can work from behind the key handling throw-ins and other assigned duties. This way a novice can gain experience without lowering the quality of the game. (See Fig. 5-1.)

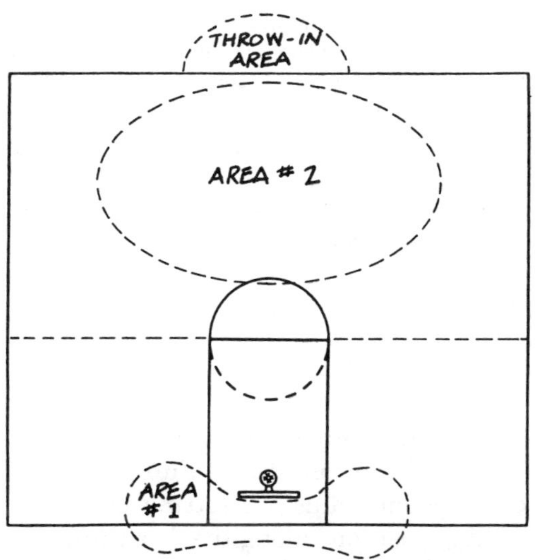

Figure 5-1. Official operates mainly in Area #1 during play. He observes throw-ins from Area #2, then moves to Area #1 when thrower-in releases the ball. When there is a second official (referee), he operates mainly in Area #2 and handles throw-ins.

Whether he is alone or part of a team, the Official stations himself at the center of the end line directly behind the basket, shifting his position according to the flow of action to maintain as unobstructed a view as possible. Although he will focus mainly on the offensive player with the ball and the defensive player who is covering him, he will attempt to keep all six players within his general view at all times. He will allow his scoring, timekeeping, and other administrative duties to occupy his attention only when the ball is dead.

The most important responsibility of the Halfcourt® Official is to keep the game moving in accordance with the principle of active offense. This is the Halfcourt® brand of "antifreeze" and takes the place of the shot clock. In making it work, the Official should follow three guidelines:

1. Watch the offensive team for failure to take advantage of opportunities to score, for lack of movement, and for movement not designed to score points.

2. Watch for slowness in following instructions, returning to the court after a time-out, clearing the front court for a free throw, assuming position for a free throw or throw-in, or entering or leaving the court for a substitution.
3. Watch for excessive questioning of calls or feigning injury.

All other duties are clearly outlined in the rules, which are unique for what they *don't* include:

1. Jump balls.
2. Lineups for free throws.
3. Individual and team foul limits.

The jump ball and lineup are eliminated to speed up the game and avoid player-Official confrontations. Full court basketball slows down to a crawl when teams are setting up for a jump ball (or rejump!) or taking positions along the free throw lane. The tradition of recreational three-on-three favors the Halfcourt® system; the game has always functioned without the jump ball and free throw. The need for an effective penalty system in Halfcourt® requires the free throw, but not the lineup.

As for foul limits, these are not required because under Halfcourt® rules there is never an advantage to fouling. And once foul limits are eliminated, there is no need to point out the offending player. "Therefore," as Earl Davis says, "there's no flak."

In all, Halfcourt® comes close to achieving the ideal of the invisible Official. Halfcourt® also offers an ideal career opportunity. Because the Official operates within a confined area, as opposed to the back-and-forth action of full court, fatigue is reduced to a minimum. An Official can handle several half-hour games in one working day and, like the Halfcourt® player, he can look forward to a lifetime of participation.

To become an accredited Halfcourt® basketball Official, it is necessary to pass a written test on the rules of Halfcourt® basketball and to work a specified number of Halfcourt® games. Applications are available through Halfcourt® Basketball Inc.

6

The Official Halfcourt® Rules for Three-on-Three Basketball

A. DUTIES OF THE OFFICIAL

1. Inspect and approve all equipment for safety and adherence to regulations.
2. Inspect and approve all uniforms for safety, adherence to regulations, clear differentiation between teams, visibility of identification, uniformity within each team, and absence of characteristics that provide unfair advantages.
3. Establish special ground rules (such as those governing low ceilings, obstructions, and irregularities in uniform markings) and inform both teams about these rules. (*Note:* It is not the duty of the Official to provide general information about the official rules of Halfcourt® basketball; this is the responsibility of the program director and coaches.)
4. Enforce all Halfcourt® basketball rules and regulations during the period starting fifteen minutes before the game and ending when the final score is approved.
5. Check and approve the score at the end of each game and sign the official scorecard.
6. Declare the end of the game.
7. Notify each team three minutes before the start of the game.
8. Notify each team when play is about to begin at the start of the game.
9. Declare the ball dead.
10. Establish first possession by a flip of a coin.
11. Signal the scoring of goals.
12. Call fouls and violations and administer penalties.
13. Call time-out.
14. Issue warnings about technical fouls and delay-of-game violations.

15. Put the ball into play on throw-ins, count the five-second throw-in time, and count aloud as each of the three offensive players touches the ball.
16. Put the ball into play on free throws and count the fifteen-second free throw time.
17. Supervise substitutions.
18. Count three-second violations.
19. Make held-ball calls.
20. Forbid practice when the ball is dead except before the game.
21. Issue instructions to maintenance and medical personnel.
22. Disqualify any player or nonplaying team member or banish any spectator for reasons specified in the rules.
23. Make clear through audible and/or visible signals the nature of foul or violation calls, the player fouled, the number of free throws, the free thrower, the team in possession, and other information needed by players, coaches, and any personnel sharing the duties of the Official.
24. Call a lineup, under the rules of substitution.
25. Accept and record (on an official Halfcourt® basketball scorecard) the names of players and coaches and the designated starting lineups at least ten minutes before the start of the game and make this information available to the opposing teams.
26. Record field goals scored.
27. Record free throws scored.
28. Keep a running total of team scores.
29. Signal and keep a record of alternate possessions.
30. Correct all errors.
31. Adjudicate all disputes and make final decisions, subject only to appeal under procedures that may exist within the league, tournament, or program.

Official's Equipment

The Official shall be equipped with:

A standard referee's whistle.

An official Halfcourt® basketball scorecard.

A clock or watch to indicate running time.

A stopwatch for one-minute time-outs before each overtime period. (The second hand of the running-time clock may be used for this purpose.)

An identifying uniform. (A black shirt with white markings is recommended.)

Division of Duties

When additional qualified individuals are available, the duties of the Official may be delegated as follows:

Scorekeeper

The Scorekeeper assumes Official duties 25 through 29. He records field goals and free throws scored *only upon the signal of the Official* (Official duties 26 and 27).

The Scorekeeper is seated at a table with an unobstructed view of the court.

The Scorekeeper is provided with an official Halfcourt® scorecard, which becomes the official record of the game.

The Scorekeeper may not call a time-out or interrupt the game. He must wait until the next dead ball to request information from the Official or call attention to any error.

The Scorekeeper notifies the Official that the game has ended if the point total is reached before running time elapses (Official duty 6), so that the Official may declare the end of the game.

The Scorekeeper is required to wear an identifying uniform.

Timekeeper

The Timekeeper maintains running time and signals the end of the game (Official duty 6) if time runs out before the point total is reached.

The Timekeeper notifies the Official by voice of all time-related responsibilities (Official duties 4, 7, 8, and 25).

The Timekeeper is seated at a table with an unobstructed view of the court.

The Timekeeper is equipped with a clock or watch and a stopwatch (see "Official's Equipment").

The Timekeeper is equipped with a sounding device to signal the end of the game.

The Timekeeper may not call a time-out or interrupt the

game. He must wait until the next dead ball to request information from the Official or call attention to any error.

The Timekeeper is required to wear an identifying uniform.

Referee

The Referee is an on-court assistant to the Official. He is stationed in the backcourt, shifting his position to maintain an unobstructed view of the action and to avoid interfering with play.

The Referee assumes all responsibility for throw-ins (Official duty 15) and any other duties that are delegated to him by the Official.

On simultaneous calls, the Official makes the final determination after consulting with the Referee. The Official makes the final determination on all interpretations of rules but may not overrule the Referee on judgment calls.

The Referee is equipped with a whistle similar to that of the Official.

The Referee is required to wear an identifying uniform.

B. TEAMS

The team roster consists of no fewer than three and no more than five players. Three players must be on the court at all times when the ball is live.

Failure to have three players on the court when the game is scheduled to begin or when the ball is live constitutes a forfeit, with one exception: If team A has three able-bodied players and one is disabled due to an intentional foul or unsportsmanlike conduct by a player on team B, the forfeit is assessed against team B.

Note: Slowness in returning to the court after a time-out or in reporting as a substitute is not a forfeit situation but may be ruled a delay-of-game violation.

C. LEAGUES AND TOURNAMENTS

Unlimited Program

Any league or tournament may be organized as an unlimited (or open) program, with no limitations as to height or age. Leagues and tournaments may also be organized as follows:

Age Divisions

Training league: Up to and including eight-year-olds. Training leagues may eliminate the three-second rule and substitute the eight-foot basket for the ten-foot basket.

Preteen leagues may be divided into two divisions:

Division 1: ages 9 and 10
Division 2: ages 11 and 12

Teen leagues may be divided into two divisions:

Division 1: ages 13–15
Division 2: ages 16–18

Adult leagues are for players nineteen and older.

Senior leagues are adult leagues with a minimum age above nineteen. Most popular are over-thirty-five and over-forty leagues.

The age of a player on the first date of competition constitutes his or her age for the entire playing schedule. Players may be placed in divisions above their age group on the basis of ability, at the discretion of the program director.

Height Divisions

Men's programs may be divided into height divisions as follows:

Division A: 6 feet and under
Division B: 6 feet 4 inches and under
Division C: Unlimited

Women's programs may be divided into height divisions as follows:

Division A: 5 feet 6 inches and under
Division B: 5 feet 10 inches and under
Division C: Unlimited

The height of a player on the first date of competition constitutes his or her height for the entire playing schedule. Players may be placed in divisions above their height group on the basis of ability, at the discretion of the program director.

Mixed Competition

In mixed competition, there must be at least two women on each roster, and each team must have at least one woman on the court at all times.

In programs organized according to age, boys and girls of the same age divisions are eligible to play together. In programs organized according to height, division A women and division A men play together, division B women and division B men play together, and unlimited women and unlimited men play together.

Intramural and Interscholastic Programs

Intramural programs are organized in accordance with the rules governing intramural sports at any given school. For example, if other sports are organized to represent grades, phys. ed. classes, fraternities, or sororities, then Halfcourt® basketball competition is organized in the same way.

In interscholastic competition, all leagues are unlimited. They may be mixed or separated by gender.

D. EQUIPMENT

The Ball

The ball is any standard basketball weighing between twenty and twenty-two ounces and measuring between twenty-nine and thirty inches in circumference, inflated as indicated by the manufacturer. The home team supplies the ball.

The Basket

The basket is the standard basketball basket, consisting of a metal ring (hoop) eighteen inches in diameter, with twelve loops from which a net is suspended. The hoop is attached to the backboard so that its top is ten feet above the playing floor and parallel to it. The center of the hoop is fifteen inches from the backboard. *Note:* The net serves to improve visibility but is not considered part of the basket in determining goaltending, throw-in, or take-back violations.

The Backboard

The preferred backboard is rectangular, seventy-two inches wide and forty-eight inches high, and made of a flat, hard surface that is either white or transparent. A fan-shaped backboard is acceptable. If the support for the backboard is on the court, it is considered out of bounds.

Uniforms

Any comfortable uniform that does not have hard, sharp, or pointed surfaces or attachments, does not distract or interfere with opposing players, and does not provide an unnatural advantage to the wearer is acceptable. The recommended uniform consists of a T-shirt or tank top, short pants, and standard sneakers.

Each player's uniform must bear a number from 1 to 5 that is plainly visible and different from the number of any other player on the same team. Players may not change their numbers during the game without informing an official before the change is made. Any other trim or decoration, such as the name of the team or player, is permissible, provided it does not cause distraction or confusion.

The home team must wear uniforms that are light in color (white, yellow, pink, sky blue, etc.), and the visiting team must wear uniforms that are dark or bright in color (navy, maroon, red, green, etc.)

The Court

The court is described in Fig. 6-1. It is the responsibility of the home team to provide the court, seating for teams, Scorekeeper and Timekeeper, proper lighting, safe conditions, crowd control,

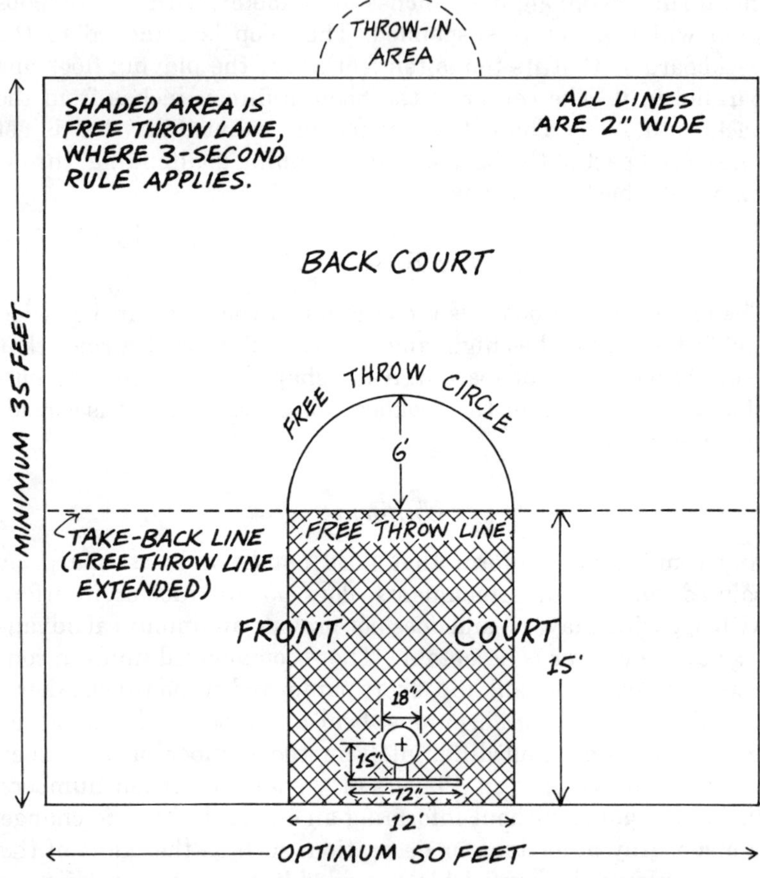

Figure 6-1. The Court—In-bounds includes all the areas inside the lines marking the perimeter of the court, and the hoop, net, and front and all edges of the backboard. Out-of-bounds includes all areas outside the perimeter of the court and the lines marking the perimeter of the court, also any backboard support or overhead obstruction, and the back of the backboard. Allow at least 3 feet of clear space around entire court for out-of-bounds activities.

security, and all other normal requirements, except as agreed upon by the league and coaches.

E. LENGTH OF GAME: THE POINT-TOTAL SYSTEM AND OVERTIME

Except for training leagues, all Halfcourt® basketball games are played to thirty points or thirty minutes of running time, whichever occurs first. (In training leagues, point totals and time limits are discretionary, with fifteen points and fifteen minutes recommended.)

If the score is tied at the end of thirty minutes' playing time, a three-minute overtime period is played. There is no point-total rule in effect during overtime. All other rules are in effect. Players or others disqualified during regular playing time may not return during overtime. Overtime begins after a one-minute time-out. Additional overtimes may be played if the game is not determined by the first overtime.

F. DELAY OF GAME: PRINCIPLE OF ACTIVE OFFENSE

In Halfcourt® basketball competition, the principle of active offense serves the same purpose that the shot clock (twenty-four-second, thirty-second, etc.) serves in full court basketball. That is, it keeps the game moving.

Under the principle of active offense, the offensive team must keep its players or the ball in active movement designed to score points. If the offensive team fails to take advantage of scoring opportunities, if there is insufficient movement, or if the movement appears designed for any other purpose than the scoring of points, the Official may call a delay-of-game violation.

There is no time limit for an active offense violation. It is based on the judgment of the Official, who should take into account the abilities of the players and the game situation.

When calling a delay-of-game penalty, the Official may:

1. Issue one or more warnings.
2. Award the ball to the defensive team.
3. Call one or more technical fouls.
4. Stop the clock.
5. Declare a forfeit.

Although these are judgment calls, it is recommended that these options be used in the above order.

Situation A

With one minute to go before the end of running time, team A has twenty-eight points and possession of the ball. Team B has twenty-six points. The Official stops the clock and allows the game to continue to the point total of thirty.

Interpretation

The situation encourages team A to freeze the ball and run out the clock. Even if that is not the intention, team A will be cautious about taking a risky shot, and the burden will be on the Official to make an almost impossible delay-of-game decision. By stopping the clock, the Official forces team A to shoot but not to take a risky shot. The game may run longer, but judging by the rate of scoring established by teams A and B, it will not run so much longer that the playing schedule will be upset.

Situation B

With one minute to go before the end of running time, team A has thirteen points and possession of the ball. Team B has twelve points. The Official allows time to run out.

Interpretation

The low score can be the result of several factors: tight defense, poor shooting, or tactics by one or both teams that slow down the game. If the cause is slow-down tactics, it is assumed that the Official has *already* imposed delay-of-game penalties sufficient to keep the game fair. In any event, stopping the clock would allow the game to run for over an hour, based on the established rate of scoring. This would upset the playing schedule and probably make excessive physical demands on the players. A one-point victory in this situation is considered equitable, because a total score of twenty-five points in thirty minutes makes each point abnormally valuable.

Situation C

Team A shows up for the game with only three players (no substitutes), while team B has a full roster of five. After ten minutes, team A is ahead by a score of fifteen to ten, but at that point the Official observes that team A is "resting" whenever it has possession of the ball, unfairly limiting team B's chances of catching up. The Official can call one or more technical fouls, or stop the clock, or both.

Interpretation

It is up to the Official to observe the effects of his first call and then make further adjustments, if necessary. For example, the Official imposes two technicals but does not stop the clock. He observes that team B has scored both of its shots, thereby demonstrating its ability to capitalize on the delay-of-game call. Team A now has the incentive to maintain a scoring pace. The Official decides that no further action is necessary (no need to stop the clock) and makes a mental note to make sure that the time taken to set up for the technical free throw is not excessive.

Question: If the clock is stopped, can it be started again? If so, where does it start?

Answer: Yes, the clock can be started again after it is stopped. Normally it picks up where it was stopped, so that no time is subtracted from the total running time. But if the clock has been stopped for a long period of time (as could happen in the case of situation C), it may be adjusted to start again with three minutes remaining, the same as an overtime period.

Question: Can the clock be stopped during overtime?

Answer: Yes, under the same circumstances as during regular time.

G. TAKING THE BALL BACK

When the defensive team gains possession of the ball during play after it has touched the backboard or hoop (following a field goal attempt, wild pass, or deflection by the offensive team), it must take the ball back behind the free throw line extended before attempting a field goal.

Taking the ball back is accomplished by bouncing the ball on any part of the backcourt (behind the free throw line), by bouncing it on the free throw line extended, or by stepping on, or in back of, the free throw line while holding the ball or controlling it on a dribble. (*Note:* If the ball touches the net but not the backboard or hoop, the defensive team is not required to take it back.)

Question: Team A captures its own rebound after the ball has touched the backboard. Then Team B steals the ball. Does team B have to take the ball back?

Answer: No. When the offensive team captures its own rebound, that is a new possession. The earlier contact of the ball with the backboard or hoop is no longer a factor. However, the offensive team must clearly gain possession, not merely touch the ball.

H. PUTTING THE BALL INTO PLAY: THE THROW-IN

The throw-in is the only way in which the ball is put into play. (There is no jump ball.) The ball is always thrown in from behind the center of the backcourt line. The thrower-in is designated by his coach or captain. The Official hands the ball to the thrower-in and blows his whistle to signal that the ball is in play. The thrower-in must release the ball within five seconds after the whistle has blown.

The thrower-in may not step onto the court or any line defining the court until he releases the ball. No other player may step out of the court or onto any line defining the court until the ball is released. The rules covering walking or traveling do not apply to the thrower-in, but he may not move more than two steps in any direction to avoid a defensive player.

The throw-in may not touch the hoop or backboard or pass through the hoop before it touches a player. No player may touch the ball before it is released by the thrower-in.

All three offensive players must touch the ball on every throw-in before a field goal is attempted. The thrower-in is *not* considered to have touched the ball on the throw-in itself. Therefore, after the throw-in pass is received, there are *two* more offensive players who must touch the ball. However, the players need not touch the ball in any special sequence, and there may be other passes and dribbles before the second and third players touch it.

Note: If the team of the thrower-in loses possession before the second or third player touches the ball, then regains possession before the next dead ball, it is *not* required that all three touch the ball before that team attempts a field goal.

I. THE FREE THROW

A player attempting a free throw may station himself anywhere behind the free throw line and within the free throw circle but not touching either the line or the circle.

The other five players on the court must position themselves behind the free throw line extended, but not within the free throw circle.

No defensive player may position himself in such a way as to distract the free thrower or make any motion or sound that may distract the free thrower.

When the players have assumed their positions, the Official gives the ball to the free thrower, who must attempt the free throw within fifteen seconds, or within a reasonable time in the judgment of the Official. If the free thrower is to attempt more than one free throw, the Official retrieves the ball and returns it to him.

On personal fouls, the free thrower is the player fouled and is designated by the Official. If he is unable to attempt the free throw because of injury or disqualification, the opposing coach or captain selects a substitute from the shooting team's roster. On technical fouls, the free thrower is selected by the coach or captain of the shooting team.

J. ALTERNATE POSSESSION AND FIRST POSSESSION

There is no jump ball. First possession in the game is determined by a flip of a coin by the Official, with the visiting team captain making the heads-or-tails call. All subsequent possessions not otherwise determined by the rules are awarded on an alternate basis. These situations include:

1. Held ball.
2. Combination defensive foul and offensive violation. (Offensive team takes free throw or throws before throw-in.)
3. Double or multiple violations by opposing teams.
4. Two opposing players touch the ball simultaneously and cause it to go out of bounds, or the Official is unsure as to which team touched the ball last.
5. The ball lodges in the basket support.
6. After a foul that occurs during a loose ball or held ball.

Overtime periods start with a new coin flip.

K. SCORING

A field goal is scored as two points. A free throw is scored as one point.

L. THE FIELD GOAL

A field goal is a successful attempt to put a live ball through the hoop from above.

A field goal may be attempted only from within the inbounds area or by a player in midair whose feet were touching the floor inbounds when he last touched the floor. The ball may touch the hoop, net, or any part of the backboard that is not out of bounds. It may not be bounced through the hoop off the floor.

After each field goal, the team scored upon is awarded possession and puts the ball into play via a throw-in.

M. THE PASS

A pass is any transfer of the ball from one player to another by throwing it with one or both hands. The ball may pass through the air without bouncing, it may bounce any number of times, or it may roll.

A pass that penetrates air space over the floor out of bounds is in play.

A player may receive a pass over the floor out of bounds while his feet are touching the floor inbounds.

A player may receive a pass while his feet are off the floor if the part of the floor they last touched was inbounds.

A player may not pass to himself, regardless of whether he is moving or stationary.

N. THE DRIBBLE

To dribble the ball, the player bounces it on the floor while he is moving or standing still. He may bounce the ball no higher than his shoulder (measured at standing height). He may start and end the dribble with one or both hands making contact with the ball, but any bounces in between must be achieved by striking the ball no more than once with the face of one open hand. He may not clutch the ball or turn it over.

The player may bounce the ball any number of times during a single dribble, and he may touch it with either hand in any sequence, but he may dribble the ball only once during each possession.

While dribbling, the player may move one or both feet, and may have both feet off the ground at the same time.

O. THE BLOCK, PICK, OR SCREEN

An offensive player may take up a stationary position either standing or crouching, with both feet on the floor and both hands either at his sides or over his head, for the purpose of blocking the movement of a defensive player. This is called a block, pick, or screen.

The player executing the block must assume his stationary position before the approaching defensive player is within two steps. After that he may not move until he is no longer in a position to affect the movement of the defensive player. The duration of the block is continuous from the time the defensive player is within two steps of the screen until he has moved out of effective range of the screen.

P. THE PIVOT AND THE PIVOT FOOT

While the player is holding the ball in one or both hands, he may move only one foot. The other foot is called the pivot foot. The pivot foot must be kept in contact with the floor in its original location, although it may be turned in place (pivoted).

The pivot foot may be raised from the floor while the player is in the act of shooting, passing, or starting to dribble. The lifting of the foot must be part of the motion of the shot, pass, or dribble.

Q. POSSESSION, HELD BALL, AND LOOSE BALL

Possession is defined differently according to the situation:

1. A team is in possession whenever a player on that team is holding the ball with one or both hands and no player on the opposing team is touching it, while the player is in the act of shooting, passing, or dribbling, and after the player has passed the ball.

2. The player who is last to touch the ball before it goes out of bounds is considered to have been in possession.
3. A held ball (both teams share possession) is called when opposing players have one or both hands so firmly on the ball that possession can be gained only by force.

Two players from the same team may not hold the ball firmly at the same time. Simultaneous touching of the ball by teammates while attempting to capture a loose ball is permitted.

A loose ball is defined as any situation in which neither team has clear possession of the ball. This includes rebounds, deflected passes and dribbles, and balls that are fumbled or accidentally kicked, which, in the judgment of the Official, both teams have an approximately equal opportunity of capturing. An undeflected pass is not a loose ball.

R. LIVE BALL AND DEAD BALL

A ball is live when it is in play and dead when play stops.

No player may practice with the ball when it is dead, except before the game.

When the ball is live, any signal by the Official's whistle makes the ball dead. *Exception:* If a whistle blows when a player is in the act of attempting a field goal, or when the ball is in flight during an attempted field goal, the ball remains live until the field goal is either successful or unsuccessful.

The ball becomes live at the signal of the Official's whistle after the Official has handed the ball to the thrower-in.

S. ZONE DEFENSE

The zone defense is permitted. There are no regulations governing the position of the defensive players in relation to the offensive players.

T. TIMEKEEPING

Fifteen-Second Rule

The free thrower is allowed fifteen seconds from the time he is handed the ball by the Official until the ball leaves his hand for the free throw attempt. The Official may allow more than fifteen seconds under extenuating circumstances, such as excessive crowd noise.

Five-Second Throw-in Rule

The thrower-in must release the ball five seconds after the whistle is blown.

Three-Second Rule

No offensive player may remain in the free throw lane for three seconds continuously. The three-second rule is not in effect while the ball is in flight during a field goal attempt, while a rebound is being contested, or at any other time when possession is unclear (loose ball).

U. SUBSTITUTIONS

Substitutions may be made whenever the ball is dead.

The most important principle of substitution is equal opportunity. Under this principle, there are three stages of substitution:

1. One team substitutes for one or two players.
2. The second team is permitted to make up to two substitutions.
3. If the second team has made one more substitution than the first, the first team may make an additional substitution. Neither team may make more than two substitutions during one dead ball.

If a player is removed for a substitute and the opposing team makes two substitutions, that player is eligible to be brought back into the game as an equalizing substitute.

Procedure

Each substitute reports to the Official by entering onto the court and calling "substitute." The Official must allow time for the replaced player to leave and for the opposing team to make its own substitution.

A team may not substitute for a player who is about to attempt a free throw, except in the event of injury or disqualification, in which case his substitute is chosen by the opposing coach or captain.

At any time when there is more than one substitution by either team, the captain or coach of either team may request a lineup. The Official may then call time-out and direct the players of each team to gather in facing lines so that their opponents may identify them.

Note: If the Official believes that lineups are being used as a delaying tactic, he may impose a delay-of-game penalty.

V. TIME-OUT

Time-out occurs when the Official blows his whistle. He may do so under the following circumstances:

To end the game or at the end of running time or overtime.
For a personal or technical foul.
For a held ball.
For a violation.
For a lineup.
For an injury (including loss of a contact lens).
When the ball lodges in the basket support.
To repair equipment.
For any emergency.

Time-out may last as long as required by the Official to accomplish his duties. *Exception:* There is a one-minute time-out before each overtime period.

Players and coaches may not request a time-out but may call

the Official's attention to an injury, obstruction, or emergency which may in *his* judgment be reason to call a time-out.

The ball is dead during time-out.

W. FOULS AND PENALTIES

Personal Fouls

A personal foul is any form of illegal contact between opposing players that occurs while the ball is in play. By definition, all forms of contact between opposing players are illegal, but in practice officials may choose not to call a personal foul for contact that does not affect the course of the game, hinder the movement of a player, cause personal injury, or serve as a distraction. This philosophy is referred to as "no harm, no foul," and its implementation is beneficial in that it helps keep the game moving.

The rules do not recognize the right of a defensive player to place his hand on an offensive player (hand checking) or the right of a player who has the inside position on a rebound to back into a player behind him.

Noncontact Fouls

There are certain personal fouls that do not involve direct physical contact but have the effect of physical contact. Such personal fouls are judgment decisions by the Official. They include, but are not limited to:

Face guarding: Keeping one's hands in front of an opponent's face so as to distract him or obstruct his vision.

Physical intimidation: Causing a player to feel threatened by implying an act of violence, including excessive swinging of the arms or legs.

Audible distraction: Making a sound so loud or unusual so as to affect the normal functioning of an opposing player, or speaking to an opposing player in a manner designed to distract him.

Contact Fouls

Personal fouls involving physical contact include, but are not limited to, pushing, tripping, hacking, holding, blocking, and charging. These terms are self-descriptive. The official signals for these fouls simulate the action of the foul (see Figs. 6-2 through 6-23).

Contact with a player also includes contact with his uniform. For example, holding a player's shirt constitutes a holding foul. Also, contact can be made by means of the ball. For example, using the ball to push a defensive player is a pushing foul.

In calling a personal foul, the Official must often make a judgment as to which player had established prior position on the floor or in air space. In making this judgment, the Official may allow no advantage to either the offensive or defensive player.

For example, when there is hand contact during an attempted field goal, the defensive player has not committed a foul if his hand was raised upward and stationary before the offensive player began the motion of his field goal attempt. In such a situation, it is the offensive player who has committed the personal foul. The principle applies even if the contact is made after the ball has left the shooter's hand.

In the case of contact between a moving player and a stationary player, the stationary player has committed a personal foul if he has stepped into the path of the moving player after he was within two steps of the point of contact or if, in the judgment of the Official, he did not give the moving player sufficient time to stop or change direction.

The stationary player also has committed a personal foul if he makes contact with an arm, elbow, or hand that is extended laterally from his body, whether the extended limb is stationary or moving.

The right of way of a moving player is extended to a player who has left the ground. For example, if an offensive player fakes a jump shot and the defensive player reacts by jumping into the air, the defensive player has the right of way in the path of his jump, unless he is jumping toward the offensive player. In simple terms, the offensive player may not cause a defensive player to leave the ground and then step in front of or under him. If he does so and there is contact, the personal foul is against the offensive player.

If a player, with or without the ball, attempts to pass between two opposing players, or between an opposing player and a teammate, or between an opposing player and an out-of-bounds line or on-court obstruction, and there is insufficient space for passage, any contact he makes with an opposing player is a personal foul.

While the hand of a player is touching the ball, that hand is considered "part of the ball." If an opposing player reaching for the ball touches that hand below the wrist he has not committed a foul.

If a player setting a pick or screen moves after the approaching defensive player is within two steps and before he is out of effective range and thereby causes contact with a defensive player or affects his movement without making contact, he has committed a personal foul. If an offensive player setting a pick or screen takes his position closer than one step from a stationary defensive player and contact or interference results, he has committed a personal foul.

If there is contact between two moving players, the official has the following options:

1. If both players are responsible, he may call a personal foul on each (double foul).
2. If one player has attempted to avoid contact and the other has not, or if contact is clearly the responsibility of one player, the Official may call a personal foul on one player.
3. If the contact does not affect the game or either player, the Official may choose to call no foul (no harm, no foul).

Double Foul

A double foul occurs when an offensive player and a defensive player commit personal fouls at approximately the same time. No free throw is awarded. The offensive team retains possession.

False Double Foul

A false double foul occurs when both teams commit personal fouls during the same sequence of action, but with time elapsed between them. Interpretation is same as for a double foul.

Multiple Foul

A multiple foul occurs when more than one personal foul is committed by one team against the other at approximately the same time. Each foul carries its own penalty and is penalized individually. If more than one player from the same team is to attempt free throws, the coach of the offended team may select the order of free throwers. If the offensive team commits more than one foul, the first foul is penalized by loss of possession and all additional fouls are penalized by free throws.

False Multiple Foul

A false multiple foul occurs when more than one foul is committed by the same team during the same sequence of action, but with time elapsed between them. Interpretation is same as for a multiple foul.

Combination Foul and Violation

If a defensive player commits a foul and an offensive player commits a violation, the offensive player takes his free throw(s) and the ball is awarded on the basis of alternate possession.

If an offensive player commits a foul and a defensive player commits a violation, possession is awarded to the defensive team (the foul outweighs the violation).

Penalties for Personal Fouls

When a defensive player fouls an offensive player, the offensive team retains possession.

If a defensive player fouls an offensive player who is not in the act of shooting (attempting a field goal), the offensive player is awarded one free throw.

If a defensive player fouls an offensive player who is in the act of shooting, the offensive player is awarded:

1. Two free throws if the field goal is unsuccessful.
2. One free throw if the field goal is successful.

If an offensive player fouls a defensive player, the defensive team is awarded possession of the ball.

Note: A field goal is nullified if the offensive team commits a personal foul before the ball has left the hands of the shooter or if the foul is the consequence of the attempted field goal.

Note: If possession is in doubt (loose ball or held ball) when a personal foul is committed, the player who is fouled is awarded one free throw; possession is then determined by alternate possession.

Two free throws are awarded for a flagrant or intentional personal foul, whether committed by an offensive or defensive player. The offensive team retains possession.

Technical Fouls

The following are technical fouls:

Creating a hazard to the safety of any player or nonplayer.
Delaying the start or continuation of the game (see "Delay of Game").
Arguing the decision of the Official.
Failure to comply with the instructions of the Official.
Kicking the ball (not including accidental contact).
Hanging from the hoop or grasping it.
Unsportsmanlike conduct.
The use of profanity.
Inciting spectators to unruly conduct.
Intentionally damaging or attempting to damage equipment.
Practicing with the ball when the ball is dead, except before the game.

Causing the backboard or basket to move to prevent or assist the scoring of a goal.

Interfering with the Official.

Having more than three players on the court.

Failure to follow the specified procedures for substitution.

Failure or delay in providing accurately any information the Official requires in order to proceed with the game.

Entering onto the court illegally.

Climbing on a teammate.

Using a basket support that is inbounds to gain advantage or to put an opposing player at a disadvantage.

Participating after disqualification or participation by an ineligible player.

Attempting a free throw that should be attempted by another player. (*Note:* After the technical foul is assessed, the correct free thrower attempts the free throw.)

Failure of a coach to provide player identifications and starting lineup to the Official ten minutes before the game, or changing uniform numbers without notifying the official, or having more than one player wear the same number. (*Note:* One free throw is awarded for each player incorrectly identified, for each player in the starting lineup who was not specified as such, and for each player more than one with the same number. Following the free throws and the correction of duplicate numbers, the corrected identifications and starting lineups shall continue as correct and official.)

Contact fouls during time out, on or off the court, that are flagrant or involve unsportsmanlike conduct.

Interference by a spectator or a group of spectators. This technical foul is assessed against the home team, unless, in the opinion of the Official, the spectators involved are supporters of the visiting team.

Penalties for Technical Fouls

Technical fouls may be called against any playing or nonplaying member of either team or against any spectator.

The penalty for a technical foul is one free throw. The Official may call any number of technical fouls at any time against either or both teams. After the free throw (or throws) has been attempted, whether successful or not, possession is retained by the team that had it when the technical foul was called.

If a technical foul and a personal foul are called at the same time, the free throw for the technical foul is attempted before the free throw for the personal foul.

The player attempting the free throw for a technical foul is chosen by the coach or captain of the shooting team.

There is no individual or team limit on technical fouls, but a player or coach may be disqualified (and a spectator may be ejected) at any time for behavior that interferes with the orderly procedure of the game. When a player or coach is disqualified, he may no longer participate in the game, he may not remain on or near the court or on or near the bench, and he may not communicate directly or indirectly with any other person involved in the game for the remainder of the game, including time-outs and overtime.

X. FORFEITS AND DISQUALIFICATIONS

The Official may declare a game forfeited for the following causes:

1. Any action by any player, nonplaying team member, or team supporter that makes it unsafe, extremely difficult, or impossible to start or complete a game, including a flagrant delay-of-game violation.
2. Any action by any player, nonplaying team member, or team supporter that creates an advantage for either team that cannot be corrected by ordinary measures or application of the rules.
3. Any action by any player, nonplaying team member, or team supporter that is extremely unsportsmanlike or offensive.
4. The failure of a team to meet the three-player requirement at the scheduled starting time or during the game.
5. An intentional or flagrant personal foul that causes an opposing player to leave the game because of injury, reducing the opposing team's roster to fewer than three, or creating a competitive disadvantage which in the judgment of the Official is critical to the outcome of the game.

6. Failure of the home team to provide adequate court and equipment.

7. Failure of either team to meet uniform requirements. Forfeit is assessed if the violation cannot be corrected.

The score of a forfeited game is the score at the time of forfeit if the forfeiting team is behind. If the forfeiting team is ahead, or if the score is tied, sufficient points are added to the total of the opposing team so that the opposing team wins by one point. All other statistics are final and official at the time of forfeit.

A player or coach may be disqualified (or a spectator may be ejected) for serious or repeated technical fouls, at the discretion of the Official.

A player may be disqualified if during the game he is found to be ineligible under league or tournament rules. (*Note:* Errors resulting from the participation of the ineligible player must be corrected; if this is not possible, the ineligible player's team forfeits the game.)

Y. VIOLATIONS AND PENALTIES

Delay-of-Game Violations

See section E.

Take-Back Violation

Failure to take the ball back (behind the foul line extended) before attempting a field goal, after having gained possession by a rebound off the hoop or backboard.

Penalty:

Loss of possession and nullification of any successful field goal. (*Note:* The violation takes place when the ball touches the backboard or hoop or passes through the hoop.)

Note: In the spirit of the take-back rule, the defense can never score for the offense. If the defense team deflects a pass or field goal attempt into the basket, the field goal is nullified, as above, and the offensive team retains possession. If a defensive player touches the ball during a successful field goal attempt but does not *cause* it to go through the hoop, it is scored as a field goal. This is a judgment call by the Official.

Throw-in Violations

The offensive team is penalized by loss of possession when the thrower-in commits any of the following violations:

1. Steps onto the court or any line defining the court before releasing the ball.
2. Fails to release the ball within five seconds.
3. Is the first to touch the ball after he has released it.
4. Moves more than two steps from his position in attempting to elude his defensive opponent(s).
5. Throws or bounces the ball so that it touches the floor or any object out of bounds before it touches another player or any part of the court inbounds.
6. Throws the ball so that it touches the hoop or backboard or passes through the hoop before touching another player or the court.
7. Hands the ball to a teammate instead of passing it, so that both touch it at the same time.

Violation: All offensive players fail to touch the ball on a throw-in before a field goal is attempted. *Penalty:* Loss of possession.

Violation: An offensive player steps out of bounds before the thrower-in has released the ball. *Penalty:* Loss of possession.

Violation: A defensive player steps out of bounds or touches the ball before the thrower-in has released it. *Penalty:* The throw-in is repeated.

Free Throw Violations

Violation: The free thrower steps on or across the free throw line or free throw circle before he releases the ball. *Penalty:* The free throw is nullified.

Violation: The free thrower fails to attempt the free throw within fifteen seconds. *Penalty:* The free throw is nullified. (If there are extenuating circumstances, such as excessive crowd noise, the Official may allow more than fifteen seconds.)

Violation: An offensive player steps into frontcourt (on the basket side of the foul line extended) or into the free throw circle before the ball is released. *Penalty:* The attempt is nullified.

Violation: A defensive player does the preceding. *Penalty:* If the attempt is unsuccessful, the free thrower is awarded another attempt. If the attempt is successful, there is no violation.

Violation: A defensive player distracts the free thrower. *Penalty:* If the free throw is unsuccessful, the free thrower is awarded a substitute free throw. If the free throw is successful, there is no violation.

Violation: Defensive and offensive violations are committed at approximately the same time. *Penalty:* Offsetting penalties; the free throw attempt counts.

Field Goal Violations

Violation: A player causes the ball to pass through the hoop from below. *Penalty:* Loss of possession, nullification of the field goal.

Violation: A player causes the ball to pass through the hoop or touch the hoop or backboard by bouncing it on the floor. *Penalty:* Loss of possession, nullification of the field goal.

Violation: A defensive player interferes with the ball on its downward flight while it is above the level of the hoop, or after it has touched the backboard and may still pass through the hoop, or while it is touching the hoop or backboard, or while any part of the ball is within the basket or within the cylinder formed by an upward extension of the hoop. This violation is defensive goaltending. *Penalty:* The field goal is scored.

Violation: An offensive player does the preceding. This violation is offensive goaltending. *Penalty:* The field goal is nullified, and the defensive team is awarded possession.

Question: Is pinning the ball to the backboard a violation?

Answer: No, unless there also is interference as described earlier.

If a player touches the ball on its downward flight, there is no violation if the ball clearly had no possibility of entering the basket.

If a defensive player touches the hoop or backboard, or reaches into the basket from above, or into the cylinder formed by an upward extension of the hoop, it is not a violation if he does it while attempting to block a dunk or stuff shot. A dunk or stuff shot is defined as a field goal attempt in which the hand (or hands) of the shooter is in continuous contact with the ball as it enters the basket or the cylinder formed by an upward extension of the hoop. The dunk or stuff shot is permissible.

Passing Violations

The penalty for any of the following passing violations is loss of possession:

1. A player receives a pass while touching the floor out of bounds or an out-of-bounds object or receives the pass while in midair after having last touched the floor out of bounds.
2. A player passes the ball to himself.
3. A player hands the ball to a teammate so that both are touching it at the same time.

Dribbling and Ball-Control Violations

The penalty for any of the following violations by a dribbler is loss of possession:

1. Dribbles more than once during a single possession. (*Note:* If another player touches the ball after it has been released, or touches and causes it to be released, or if the dribbler catches his own rebound, any of these conditions constitutes a second possession, and the dribbler may dribble again.)
2. Bounces the ball higher than his shoulder (measured at standing height).
3. Strikes the ball with a closed hand.
4. Touches the ball with both hands at the same time, except at the beginning or end of the dribble.
5. Clutches the ball or turns it over.
6. Controls the ball with a part of his body other than the hand.

Traveling Violation

Violation: A player moves both feet while holding the ball. *Penalty:* Loss of possession. (*Note:* There is no violation if the pivot foot is turned in place or if the lifting of the pivot foot off the ground is in the uninterrupted act of shooting or passing or starting to dribble.)

Timekeeping Violations

Fifteen-second violation: See "Free-Throw Violations."

Five-second violation: See "Throw-in Violations."

Three-second violation: An offensive player remains in the free throw lane for three seconds continuously while his team has clear possession and the ball is not in flight during a field goal attempt. *Penalty:* Loss of possession.

Question: Does the three-second rule apply to a player whose team has gained possession as the result of a rebound but has not yet taken the ball back?

Answer: Yes. By gaining possession the team has become the offensive team, even though it is not yet eligible to attempt a field goal.

Out-of-Bounds Violations

Violation: A player causes the ball to go out of bounds or is the last player to touch it before it goes out of bounds. *Penalty:* Loss of possession.

Violation: A player touches the out-of-bounds line or a person, object, or part of the floor that is out of bounds while he has possession of the ball. *Penalty:* Loss of possession. (*Note:* If a dribbler steps out of bounds between bounces of the ball, this is a violation even if he is not touching the ball while his foot is out of bounds.)

Violation: A player touches the ball while in midair, having been out of bounds when he left the floor. *Penalty:* Loss of possession. This is a violation regardless of where the player lands. The point last touched determines whether he is inbounds or out of bounds.

Violation: An offensive player makes progress out of bounds. *Penalty:* Loss of possession. The offensive player must reenter the court at the point where he left it.

Violation: A defensive player gains possession by making progress out of bounds. *Penalty:* Loss of possession.

Violation: The ball passes over the top of the backboard from front to back or back to front. *Penalty:* The team that touched the ball last loses possession. This rule applies to both rectangular and fan-shaped backboards. (*Note:* A ball moving parallel to the end line that passes over or behind the backboard is not in violation.)

Violation: A defensive player and an offensive player who has possession of the ball make contact in such a way as to cause the offensive player to step out of bounds (this is a "force-out"). The defensive player has committed a violation. *Penalty:* The offensive player retains possession. (*Note:* The force-out ruling permits an equitable call in place of a personal foul in situations as described here.)

Note: Out of bounds is defined as part of the floor or any object that is outside the inbounds edge of the line that marks the perimeter of the court; the back of the backboard; any backboard support, including a support that is anchored to the floor inbounds; and any overhead obstruction, including ceiling and lights.

Double and Multiple Violations

If one or more violations are committed by both teams at the same time or approximately the same time, alternate possession is awarded.

If more than one violation is committed by one team at the same time or approximately the same time, only the more serious violation is penalized.

Z. CORRECTING ERRORS

Errors may be corrected until the final score is approved. Corrections should nullify any unfair advantage within the limits of available information and practicality. Corrections may include the changing of the score, the administering of technical fouls, disqualification of a player, or any other measure that is equitable and serves the purpose. In correcting errors, the Official may use any source of information that is considered reliable.

AA. ABBREVIATED HALFCOURT® BASKETBALL RULES

The following abbreviated Halfcourt® basketball rules are distributed to players participating in programs sanctioned by Halfcourt® Basketball Inc. They may not be reproduced without permission of HBI.

1. *Delay of Game.* Any of the following violations may be penalized by a warning, technical foul, loss of possession, a combination of these penalties, or forfeit, at the discretion of the Official:

a) Failure by the offensive team to take advantage of scoring opportunities, lack of movement by the offensive team, or movement not designed to score points.
b) Slowness in following the Official's instructions, when entering or leaving the court, or when taking position for a throw-in or free throw.
c) Excessive questioning of the Official or feigning injury.

2. The game will start with a flip of coin for possession. There is no jump ball. All possessions not otherwise decided by the rules will be decided by alternate possession, starting with the team that wins the flip of the coin.

3. The throw-in spot will be behind the backcourt line. On a throw-in, all three players must touch the ball before a field goal is attempted.

Note: The thrower-in must touch the ball again after stepping inbounds. The throw-in counts as a touch only for the player receiving the pass.

4. The ball is put into play after each field goal by the team scored upon.

5. When a try for a field goal is recovered by the defense *after the ball touches the backboard or hoop*, that team must take the ball back behind the foul line extended before attempting a goal. In taking the ball back, either the ball or the foot of the player in possession must touch the foul line extended or the area behind it.

If the defense steals the ball or recovers a try for goal that *does not touch the backboard or hoop*, that team may attempt a goal without taking the ball back.

6. The Official will handle the ball on all out-of-bounds plays.

7. Rosters: Up to five (5) players per team (3 starters, 2 substitutes).

8. The ball is dead after a foul or violation is called or a field goal is made, and at any other time when the Official sounds his whistle.

9. Substitutions may be made on a dead ball. When one team makes a substitution the other team must be given an opportunity to substitute. Players entering the game must report by calling the word "substitute" to the Official.

10. *Fouls*—General Rules: No harm, no foul. No line-up during free throw. All nonshooting players remain in backcourt.

Penalties:

a) Foul on a missed field goal attempt—Two free throws, offensive team keeps possession.
b) Foul on a successful field goal attempt—One free throw, offensive team keeps possession.
c) Offensive player is fouled while not attempting a field goal—One free throw, offensive team keeps possession.
d) Loose ball foul—One free throw, possession is determined by alternate possession.
e) Technical foul—One free throw, no change of possession.
f) Defensive player is fouled—Defensive team gains possession.

Notes:

There are no individual or team foul limits, as the foregoing rules take away any advantage in committing a personal foul.

Definition of a personal foul: Any contact that affects the course of the game, or any noncontact activity, such as face guarding or shouting, that affects the course of the game.

Definition of a technical foul: Unsportsmanlike conduct, actions that may cause injury, delay of game, a flagrant personal foul that is committed while the ball is dead, illegal use of the basket support.

Referee's options: The Referee may issue a warning instead of a technical foul, or may disqualify a player instead of issuing a warning or technical foul at his discretion, regardless of the number of technical fouls previously called.

11. The winning team is the first team to score 30 points, or the team with the high score after 30 minutes of running time. If there is overtime, it will commence with a flip of coin for possession. The overtime period is three minutes.

12. No time-outs will be called by either team. A player's injury time-out is called by the Official. The clock continues running. *The Official may stop the clock at his discretion, and is advised to do so at any time if allowing the clock to run gives either team an unfair advantage.*

13. The uniform prescribed by the program director must be worn at all games and may not be altered.

14. Time limits:

a) For an offensive player in the free throw lane—3 seconds. Penalty—loss of possession.
b) For a thrower-in to release the ball—5 seconds. Penalty—loss of possession.
c) For a free thrower to release the ball—15 seconds. Penalty—the free throw is nullified.

15. A held ball is called when opposing players have one or both hands so firmly on the ball that possession can be gained only by force. The ball is awarded on the basis of alternate possession (see Rule 2).

16. Forfeit time is game time. Three players must be on the court ready to play.

17. On those courts where the basket support is on the playing court, a player whose body touches the support is not considered out of bounds, unless he has control of the ball. If the ball touches the support, it is considered out of bounds. No player may use the support to gain advantage or put an opposing player at a disadvantage.

BB. MODIFICATIONS OF OFFICIAL HBI RULES FOR SPECIAL OLYMPICS

1. Games will be played to fifteen points or fifteen minutes (instead of thirty points or thirty minutes).
2. Coaches may call two twenty-second instructional time-outs (instead of no time-outs).
3. All players present must participate in the game.
4. Divisions are set up according to a skills test, which will consist of a five-minute game in which all players must play (instead of divisions set up according to age and gender).

CC. OFFICIAL SIGNALS

The Official should clarify his calls verbally and with additional hand signals, which he may improvise. The whistle is used only to start and stop play and to start and stop the clock, as indicated by the hand signals that accompany the whistle. The Official counts aloud as each offensive player touches the ball on the throw-in, but this voice signal is not accompanied by a hand signal.

Figure 6-2. Start clock (blow whistle).

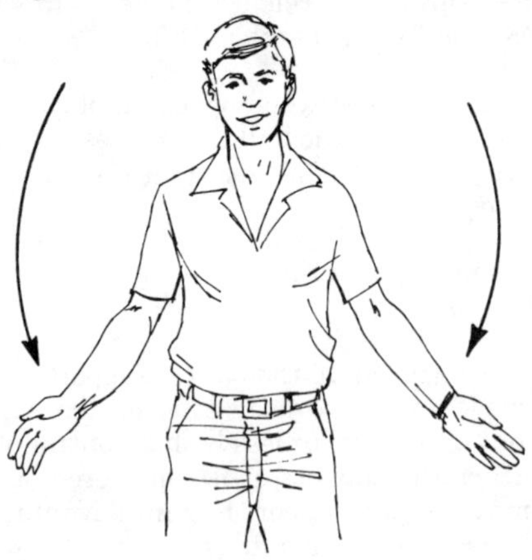

Figure 6-3. Stop clock (blow whistle).

Figure 6-4. Stop play, ball is dead (blow whistle).

Figure 6-5. Start play, ball is live (blow whistle).

Figure 6-6. Delay of game.

Figure 6-7. Alternate possession.

Figure 6-8. Score the goal.

Figure 6-9. Nullify the goal.

Figure 6-10. Bring in the substitute.

Figure 6-11. Points scored, 1 or 2. Also indicates number of free throws.

Figure 6-12. Personal foul or violation. Follow with descriptive signal.

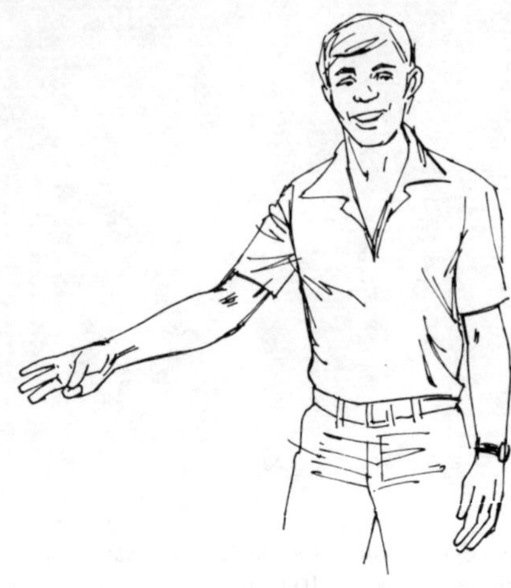

Figure 6-13. 3-second foul violation.
5 fingers for
5-second throw-in violation.

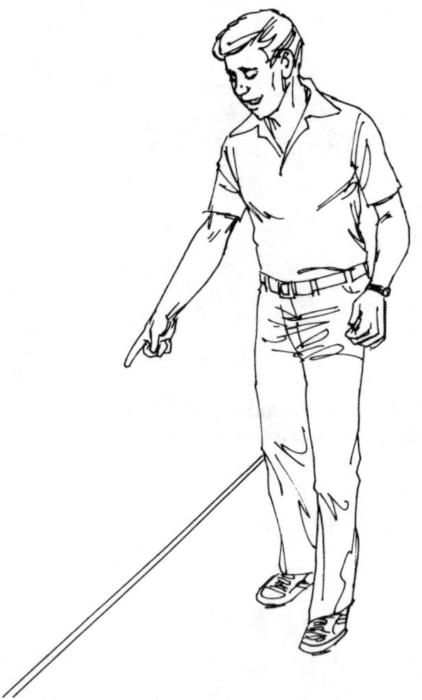

Figure 6-14. Out-of-bounds violation.
Also indicates: Take the ball out
(point to team or player in
possession) and take-back violation
(point to take-back line).

Figure 6-15. Dribbling violation.

Figure 6-16. Traveling violation.

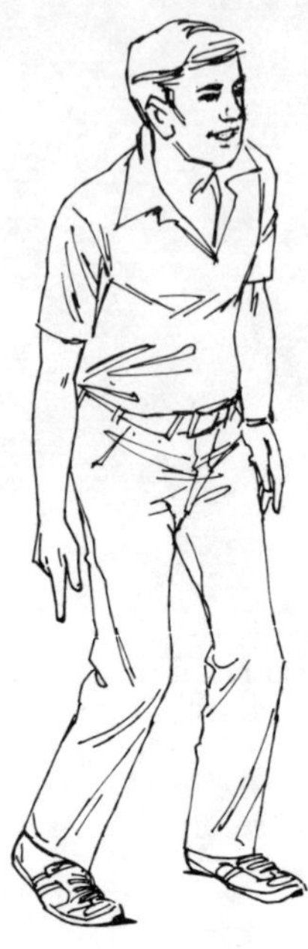

Figure 6-17. Illegal use of foot: Foul or violation.

Figure 6-18. Player control (offensive) foul.

Figure 6-19. Pushing or charging foul.

Figure 6-20. Holding foul.

Figure 6-21. Illegal use of hands foul.

Figure 6-22. Blocking and pushing foul.

Figure 6-23. Technical foul.

Index